# CAUTION:

# THIS VEHICLE MAKES FREQUENT STOPS FOR BOILED PEANUTS

SEAN DIETRICH

ISBN-13: 978-1532887765

ISBN-10: 1532887760

# DEDICATION

To my wife. May she keep her sassy attitude until my
final breath.

# ACKNOWLEDGMENTS

To all the folks who read my writings every morning on Facebook, or my blog, thank you. It is because of your support and love that I'm even taking the time to compile these stories into book format. I'll be honest, words fail me. So I'll just say, thanks. And thank you once again.

# CHOICES

I tried to buy beer yesterday and nearly had a nervous breakdown when I saw the overwhelming selection. Remember when we only had three beers to choose from? Budweiser, Miller, and Busch? Today, there are one hundred fifty-six different brands at Piggly Wiggly.

I asked the supermarket attendant where the regular Busch was. He took me out back and said, "Most of us boys go behind that bush, right there."

So, I went.

What about the soup aisle? As a boy, we had five kinds of Campbell's to choose from. Chicken Noodle, Cream of Mushroom, Clam Chowder, and a can of tomato-flavored battery acid—customarily served with grilled cheese. Not today. Modern soups have become exotic.

Just last week, my wife came home from the store with soup flavors I'd never heard of. Rice Noodle Mung, Stewed Kale, and Cream of Goat's Foot.

I can't eat my grilled cheese with stewed kale. It's an affront to the way I was raised.

The truth is, all these choices have ruined customer satisfaction. With too many options, I'm afflicted by buyer's remorse the moment I choose one laundry soap over another. What happened to the limitations of yesteryear?

Like blue jeans.

Long ago, jeans were horrid things. Not at all like today's pants. They didn't fit you like a glove, not until you'd worn them for two years. No, when you first bought them, they were dark, stiff, and cut off the circulation to your unmentionables. And we enjoyed our ugly Levis. Because, we're Americans, dammit. We have a long history of being stuck with things we don't want and complaining until we learn to adjust.

That's life.

And it's why our forefathers drank beer.

# SCATTERED

It was seven in the morning when we scattered Daddy's ashes on the mountainside. He requested to be packaged in a cardboard box instead of an urn. "Don't put me in a fancy vase," he said once. "Those things're expensive. Besides, I want you to scatter me."

Well, cremated ashes don't scatter. I thought when we turned Daddy loose, something marvelous would happen. Maybe a gust of wind would carry him across the mountains.

No.

He chose the mountains for his resting place. That was where he wanted to be; whether alive or dead. "I'm a Virgo," he said once. "Virgos love mountains."

"What's a Virgo?" I asked.

"Hell if I know, I heard it on television."

"Well if you're a Virgo, what am I?"

"You?" He laughed. "You're a Baptist."

My daddy took me mountain-camping more than I cared for. Together, we explored Longs Peak, Pikes Peak, Elbert, Crestone, Cold Mountain, Stone Mountain, Blood Mountain, Mount Mitchell, and handfuls more. And whenever we climbed four feet above sea-level, I would turn eggplant-purple and slip into oxygen debt. Which is what happens to Baptists.

3

At Daddy's mountainside memorial, we fell silent. We sliced open his plain box—I've seen UPS parcels that looked more reverent. There were no gusts of wind from On-High. No music. In fact, Daddy wasn't even proper dust, he was more like clay. His remains fell seven-hundred feet down the cliffside, tumbling like a brick, then shattered.

"Oh my God." Mother covered her mouth. "He's really gone."

But he wasn't gone. He was there. In the mountains.

And then I threw his empty box in the trash.

# LOVE SONGS

"Call today," said the television announcer, at two in the morning. "Order all the country hits from the fifties and sixties. Including the love songs you remember." Then they played through a barrage of melodies that are stuck in my head even now.

Love songs. What happened to them? I want to know what teenagers have done with the world's love music. And I'm talking about real ones, not songs about knocking boots in Nashville. I speaking of tunes like, "Can't Help Falling In Love With You," or the immortal George Jones', "He Stopped Loving Her Today," which always makes me cry.

After a few weeks, Time Life mailed me eighteen CDs with two hundred seventy-eight country songs. I played them during a seven-hour drive to Georgia while eating chili-cheese Fritos.

The first song to grace my stereo was, "Crazy." Then, "Gentle On My Mind," followed by, "Okie From Muskogee." You might not even know these songs, but that's not important. They're tender tunes, sweetly sung, with melodies that make you smile.

When I reached Lake City, "Blue Eyes Crying in the Rain." By Jacksonville, I was singing along with Willie Nelson. Then, in my dark windshield, I could almost see my mother and daddy slow dancing in our den to, "Tennessee Waltz," and "Faded Love."

Look, I don't mean to be critical. But truth is, modern music isn't about love. Hormonal adolescents have taken over our world, and then they quit wearing underpants. They sport sunglasses indoors and use verbs I've never heard. George Jones is dead, and Willie looks a little less pink every day.

I suppose my grandmother was right when she said, "Today's society isn't interested in love. And, son, when folks quit singing about love, beware. That ain't a world you want to live in."

Well, we're not there yet, Grandmama, but you'd be awfully disappointed in us.

Because we're pretty damn close.

# RALPH

Ralph was a decent fella. He smoked like a fish, and he cussed so that the hair on my neck curled—but he was decent.

We worked together, as house painters. If you've ever painted, you'll understand painting an eighty-eight-year-old woman's living room is possibly the worst torture conceived by man. When we finished rolling her room, the woman hobbled out to inform us her walls were not as "minty" green as the sample had indicated. And since mint green was only a concept, we didn't argue.

Ralph had the patience of Job. He went to the store, purchased another shade, and we painted the whole interior again, no charge. It took another full day. And it bears mentioning: there is no earthly-damn reason for eighteen-foot vaulted ceilings. It is a waste of God's oxygen, painting them is cruel and unusual punishment.

We finished the room with Italian-Parsley green. The woman took one look and wagged her head. "This is wrong," she said. "This is not the color I paid for."

Dear Ralph took a deep breath and tightened his lips.

We drove into town for twenty gallons of Winter-Asparagus green, which looks a lot like day-old cat vomit mixed with Italian parsley.

I asked Ralph why he was being so tolerant. I would've told the lady to go make toast in her bathtub two days ago.

"Nah," said Ralph. "This lady reminds me of my mother. She's lonely. We're the most company she's had in years. She don't want us to leave."

"But, you're losing money."

He shrugged. "Some things are more important than money."

Like an exact shade of green.

And people.

# SHE LEAKS

Two days ago, I saw an old truck at a traffic light. There was no mistaking it. A red, oil-leaking, '79 Chevy, with a mutilated rear bumper, and a dent on the tailgate the size and shape of a mailbox. It used to be mine, before I sold it long ago.

The new owner glanced at me, flicked his cigarette into the road, then rolled up his window.

It was a good little truck. I bought it with a shoebox of cash, from a man in Straughn, Alabama, who told me upfront, "She leaks oil."

"Don't we all, sir," I replied. "It's no problem."

Well, it turned out to be a big problem. Every driveway I ever blessed, bore an irregular-shaped black splotch, making me famous with the girls.

Once, I slept in that truck. Behind a church in Franklin, Tennessee. The next morning, I donned a necktie, and watched my friend get married.

As a young man, I drove the truck to job-sites. I learned to lay tile, brick, hang gutter, and build decks. During which period, I also learned to confront dishonest employers. And once, while shoved against the hood of that truck, I learned how to take a whipping from a boss twice my age.

In that '79 Chevy, I learned how to open passenger-doors for ladies in heels. I also discovered not everyone in this world is looking for love. No, the truth is, some folks don't know what they're looking for. Whatever it is, it sure as hell isn't love.

When the light turned green, Little Red charged forward, same as it used to. I can't believe it's lasted this long. It always was a sturdy thing, by God. A lot stronger than I ever gave it credit for.

And I'm not talking about the truck.

# SUNDAY PAPERS

If you have five extra dollars in your pocket, consider tipping the newspaper deliveryman. If you don't subscribe to the paper, tip your mail carrier. Or anyone, for that matter.

You might end up tipping someone like Eddie, my old coworker. A single father with three girls at home. He was glad to show you their wallet photograph if you had a second.

Eddie and I both threw the newspaper.

If you've never thrown the paper, here's how it works:

Imagine fourteen hundred pounds of Sunday coupons stacked in a pile roughly the size of a Waffle House. Then, shove sixty thousand of them into cigar-sized plastic sleeves. Crank down your windows. Now drive in circles through the rain—and toss. Do this for seven hours, then reward yourself with an oil change.

Eddie worked like a refrigerator. After a morning of deliveries, he stocked shelves at Walmart. When he finished there, he took a nap. After that, he did it all over again.

"It ain't so bad," said Eddie. "I sleep in my car, so I have extra minutes with my girls. I hardly get to see them."

The backseat of Eddie's car was a walk-in closet and pantry combined. Hanging clothes, sneakers, boxes of crackers, beef jerky, drinking water, and Mountain Dew.

Eddie explained, "Used to, I'd sleep at gas stations, but cops don't like that. Nowadays, I park in used car lots. They can't find me there."

I'm sure you're practically invisible, Eddie.

He went on, "Mostly, my oldest girl takes care of the younger two. She's fifteen, smart as a whip. God, I miss them." He reached for his wallet. "I have a picture of my girls, right here. Wanna see them?"

Don't be silly, Eddie, of course I want to see them.

And so do you.

# SOUTHERNGLISH

I saw it on the news; they've started teaching Southern English in grade schools. It's only fair. Because ever since the Army wore knickerbockers, kids have learned Yankee-Doodle English.

Children used to be taught that "chair" had one syllable. Well, anyone from the Yellowhammer state knows better. It has two. So do words like: floor, fire, and bed.

Let's talk about cussing. Northerners don't cuss right, they use the F-word like an assault rifle. But when a Southerner swears, it sounds a lot like Andy Griffith reading the Psalms.

How about the S-word? Southerners finesse it. "Shee-yet." When Yankees use it, they sound like Hitler giving a wedding toast.

Furthermore, the S-word doesn't mean the same thing down in Dixie. Here, it means something akin to, "We missed you at the men's fellowship last night."

There are also words in the deep South, commonly slurred so fast you might miss them. Words like, "fittna."

Example: "I'm fittna go home in a few minutes."

The word: "ah-ite." Example: "Sister So-And-So has been sick as a dawg. Gaw, I hope she's feeling ah-ite."

Or: "mo-kana." As in: "My pants aren't white, but mo-kana grayish."

And the onomatopoeic: "Pssshht." Which means: "You are dead to me."

Then there are words whose Southern definitions are unclear. Words like, "yonder." In Georgia, for instance, yonder means: wherever the hell I point.

And: "just the other day," which refers to any date occurring after the birth of Christ.

Also, I'm tired of jokes with the cute catchphrase, "bless your heart." Contrary to popular belief, that's not a backhanded insult. God no. A real Southern jab goes something like: "Isn't she just precious?" Or: "Oh, I love your haircut, it really slims your face." Or the worst Cotton State insult of all time: "That poor girl, we pray for her in Bible study every week."

Which is downright god-awful.

And you better hope to hell it ain't true.

# MAKE A WISH

You don't want to read this. Because today's my birthday, and I'm liable to say anything that comes to mind.

Right now, I'm going to make one of those god-awful speeches like they do at the Academy Awards. You know, the kind that ends with something like: "I love you momma, you believed in me when no one else did!"

You might as well quit reading right here.

Cue the music.

First off: Andrew, who introduced me to beer. God bless you, my boy. To the Eudora Wildcats, for allowing me to hit the only grand slam of my career. A story I still tell today—even though it was only tee-ball.

To my grandmother, whose head rests on an embroidered pillow that reads: "I love you Grandma." To Daddy, who didn't even say goodbye before he died. He must've thought I was strong enough to handle it. Maybe I was.

To my sister: you're going to be a great mother.

Thanks Melissa, for being a candle in a foggy

world.Lanier: for teaching me how to watch Lifetime Television for Women.

And thank you God. For introducing me to Lyle. Thank you Lyle, for introducing me to Sherry. And thank you Sherry and Lyle, for introducing me to fried calamari.

Thank you to my wife, Jamie, for pimento cheese. For homemade biscuits. And for just this morning, pointing out a barely-visible-to-the-naked-eye, microscopic white hair in my beard.

And for once telling me, "You are impulsive, irrational, your feet smell, and you talk too much. But, I think I'd like to marry you, Sean Dietrich."

And of course. I'd be remiss if I didn't thank someone else. A five-foot-tall woman, with iron between her ears, and cotton in her heart. Who has always believed in me.

Even when no one else did.

# JUST QUIT IT

I am going to die; my doctor told me to give up bacon. He made me hold up my right hand and swear it. But you should know upfront: I can't keep those kinds of promises. I'm not built for it.

The first dietary resolution I ever made was at age twelve. It happened one day at the public pool. I removed my shirt and heard giggling.

It was thereupon, Pauline Meadows said I resembled a tube of biscuit dough that'd been smacked firmly against the counter. My peers thought that was hysterical.

In effort to slim up, I resolved to quit drinking Coca-Cola until Jesus came back. But unfortunately, he took too long.

Over the years, I've quit drinking Coke several times. I've sipped diet soda in its place, but that stuff makes me gag. I've tasted commercial toilet cleaners with more personality.

Giving up Coke is almost as difficult as coffee. Have you ever tried kicking that habit? My first morning without coffee, I peeked into the mirror and saw the face of an anemic Mick Jagger looking back at me. To be fair, things did get better. Because as it turns out, if you substitute coffee with Mountain Dew, you feel like a hummingbird.

The thing is, I can't give up bacon, butter, ham, Coca-Cola, or coffee. At least not altogether.

For as long as I've peed in the upright position, I've eaten bacon. My mother cooked fatback slices as soon as the sun came up. After which, she'd fry eggs, sausage, and hash browns in the same skillet. Then, she'd pour the stiffest cup of black coffee legal in three counties.

After my light breakfast, I'd strut my hindcheeks to the public pool, buy a Coke, strip down to my skivvies, then jump into the shallow end.

And play Marco Polo with anorexia victims.

# COPYCATS

I had a friend who almost drove me to the brink of insanity. He did everything the same way I did it. The same damn way. He even combed his hair like me. But to be fair, I've decided not to tell you his name, or else he might get pathetically embarrassed. And we wouldn't want that.

Anyway, one day the friend I was just referring to, Andrew Milligan Kerley, said to me, "Hey, are you going to the roller derby costume party?"

Going? There was no question about it. In fact, I'd spent five years perfecting my outfit for it—which was top secret. I was going as the Scarecrow from the Wizard of Oz. And the reason I'd chosen such a costume was because Molly Baker was famously going as Dorothy.

And I loved Molly Baker.

"You bet your donkey I'm going," I told Andrew.

"You bet your donkey I'm going, too," copied Andrew.

I placed my hand on his shoulder. "Don't copy me, Andrew, it's rude."

He placed his hand on my shoulder. "Sorry."

I sighed and shook my head.

So did he.

The night of the skating party, kids dressed up to beat the band. There were costumes of all shapes and sizes. Robots, sailors, princesses, cowboys, and soldiers.

And then I saw her. Molly Baker. She stood in the corner, looking as cute as a stick of butter, the spitting-image of Dorothy.

But before I could even lace up my skates, something shot past me. Andrew Milligan Kerley, pathetically dressed as the Scarecrow. He rolled right up to Molly and made a grand bow.

Later that night, I sat outside on the curb, mumbling obscenities to myself. Words that would've landed a boy in prison. That's when Andrew's daddy pulled up in a rust-covered Pontiac.

He hopped out, stumbling like a fool. He took one look at me and giggled. "Hey, boy," he said. "Your momma sent me here to pick you up, you little brat."

Then, he fell limp against his truck and lit a cigarette.

"You've got the wrong scarecrow," I said.

He eyed me up and down."Well I'll be damn, son, Andy must think a lot of you then."

I made a face.

"Shoot," he said. "Andy and his momma spent a whole week putting his stupid costume together, just so he could look like you. His hero."

"Hero?"

Andrew's daddy laughed until smoke wafted out of his nose. "Oh, he's a pathetic little shit."

"No sir." I shook my head. "You've got the wrong scarecrow again."

Because now you're referring to me.

# RESOLUTIONS

Well I'll be damned. One study found this year's most popular New Year's resolution is to travel more. Which might sound like a fabulous thing, except the statistic is dead-wrong.

At least in the South it is.

Because if you measured just Southerners, you'd find only three percent want to travel more. Meaning: there's not enough Southerners with wanderlust to form a gospel quartet.

What can we say? We like it here.

Don't get us wrong, Southerners enjoy sightseeing like anyone else. We just don't need to leave the South to do it, thank you very much.

We have Charleston, South Carolina. The world's most historic city—second to Rome. Sure, Rome might have naked sculptures, but so does Charleston. And George Washington never slept in the Colosseum did he? No. But he slept in the John Ruteledge house— probably naked. They all did back then. My wife and I slept in Georgie's exact bed.

Only, on top the covers.

Savannah's marvelous, too. Once, we stayed at a haunted hotel, which made my wife nervous. I paid the eight-year-old boy next door five dollars to make ghost noises and beat on the walls from time to time. And that is how I broke two ribs.

Interested in exotic foods? Go to Chipley, Florida for a possum fry. Try the tail. You want beaches? Orange Beach, Alabama. Mountains? Banner Elk, North Carolina. Hiking? Virginia. Music? New Orleans. I could do this all day.

No. We're not all world travelers. Go ahead, call us narrow minded, we've been called worse at the Iron Bowl. Small-town Southerners aren't like everyone else. They don't need to wake up in Alexandroupoli, Greece to find themselves.

We're not not running from anything, and we sure as hell aren't chasing it, either. We're family people, churchgoers, artists, fishermen, millworkers, and cooks. We don't need passports to discover what we already have. Maybe you do.

Well.

Maybe you ought to come down here and pay us a visit.

# NEW YEAR

Mllions of years ago, New Year's Eve was a rather disappointing thing. Way back then, our filthy ancestors huddled around campfires, sipping swamp water, grunting at teenagers who peed too close to camp. Then, after midnight, they'd dig a hole in the forest, and moan, "Uggh!" Which loosely translates into: "I wish someone would hurry up and invent a fiber supplement."

And for millennia that's how things went.

Well, sometime after the dawn of Metamucil, New Year's turned into a time for tequila, Jägermeister, and making grand resolutions.

One psychologist explains, "New Year's resolutions set people up for disappointment. Each year they realize how little they've accomplished. In a single word: people feel like miserable failures."

I wish someone would've told that quack that was two words.

Last New Year's Eve, I sat at the bar. And before the bartender would allow me a beer, she said, "No drinks until you tell me your resolution."

I said I didn't have one. So she curtly swatted my knuckles with a ruler. "Don't you want to accomplish anything, loser?"

Of course I do. But, there's a lot of pressure on us. We're all supposed accomplish a lot. We're expected to keep in shape, be financially savvy, eat organic, reply to texts, trim our nails, exercise, and eat plenty of fiber.

Well, consider Jonah: a ten-year-old who lives in a cardboard box with his daddy in Mobile. When asked what Jonah wanted to accomplish this year, he said, "To find a microwave, so we can eat hot food sometimes."

I don't care if the bartender slaps the hell out of my knuckles, I don't want anything this year.

Except for Jonah to get his microwave.

# A SOUTHERN LADY

You'd never know she doesn't have a pair of breasts beneath that bra. But she doesn't.

"I don't want fake ones," she told me. "Not inside me. Something about it feels strange. Maybe it's because my mother was a proper Southern lady, I don't know. "

Well, this Southern lady is forty-three now. Five years ago, she went in for a routine check-up. It was bad. After the doctors diagnosed her, she cried in bed for a whole week. Treatment changed her appearance. Her two daughters didn't know what the hell was going on, or why their mother looked so sickly.

"I didn't want my girls to know," she said. "I'd leave for therapy, and tell them I was going out for a manicure. They'd get upset." She gave a laugh. "They wanted to get their nails painted, too."

She tried to do everything she could to salvage her breasts, but physicians warned against it. Some things aren't worth keeping, not when they're killing you.

Not when you have daughters.

"Before you get sick," she explained. "You never

think about things like this. You can't imagine body parts you're proud of, as a woman, are killing you." She glanced at her own chest. "Even though I knew it was the right thing, I wasn't ready to lose them."

The surgeon performed a full mastectomy, removing what she described as her most prized female possessions.

She went on, "When I first looked at myself in the mirror, I felt like a ten-year-old boy. The week after my procedure, I broke down and told my girls what'd happened. We all cried."

Well, it's been five years. She's cancer free—knock on wood.

She wiped her eyes and said, "My two girls have developed breasts of their own now. I'm really glad I'm still alive for that, I know that must sound silly to you."

No ma'am. It's not silly. Not to me.

And not to your daughters.

# THESE ARE MY PEOPLE

I never knew I belonged to a clan, but I do. It took me a long time to figure out who they were. In fact, you might even be one of us. But if you're not already a member, I'll go ahead and tell you about our organization.

For starters:

We cry at songs. Poetry too. We believe in babies, the elderly, well-told jokes, dogs, cats, crickets, and long bouts of quiet. We doubt ourselves, but we doubt you even more.

We make awful spouses and lifelong lovers. Horrible children, but good sons and daughters. Above all, we enjoy the idea of God; because there aren't any better ones out there.

At night, we lay in bed and consider how delicate our own rib cages are. Like raw chicken bones. Our itty-bitty hearts, too. And even though someone like you might never think about things like that, some of us do, and have for decades.

The thing is, we wonder what death feels like, and

why it hasn't kicked us yet. What the hell makes us so lucky?

But I'm breaking the rules. We don't generally talk about these things with non-members. Lord, no. Because you'd end up thinking we were terribly depressive. In fact, that's what you're thinking now.

But we're not as sad as you think.

The truth is, we're a lot like you, except, we've lost someone. We were unlucky enough see it. We pressed our ears against their chicken-bone ribs, while holding their rigor-mortised hands. We cussed God Himself out because He was the only one who could take it. We tossed handfuls of dirt on seven-foot boxes and mumbled half-assed eulogies. We slept for weeks, lost weight from malnutrition, and sobbed so hard we vomited.

We're a clan.

Our stories are different, but we recognize fellow members without saying nary a word. We're not sick. We're strong, dammit. For each other.

One day you'll understand everything I just wrote here.

And when that happens, we'll be strong for you, too.

# YES MA'AM

I shouldn't write this. Because what I'm about to tell you comes from eavesdropping. Which is admittedly wrong, and something my mother discouraged.

But.

I found myself in the department store dressing room trying on jeans. In the cubicle next to mine was an eleven-year-old boy having a rough day. I'll call him, Tyler.

Something you should know: the last thing eleven-year-old boys want is to go shopping with their mothers. Because mothers tug on your belt and say things like, "Come give momma a kiss, you special little handsome man." Or worse, they'll insult your fashion sensibilities.

Like Tyler's mother.

"Tyler," his mother henpecked. "Why on earth did you pick that god-awful shirt?"

To which Tyler responded in earnest, "I dunno."

"Do you even like this shirt?"

Tyler decided to restate his faithful adage.

"Well, I won't have you wearing that to school, or

else we'll be the laughing stock of town."

And then, Tyler unwittingly dug his own grave. "But Mother, the popular boys wear these."

"Tyler," she answered. "Popularity is like whiskey. People tell you if you wear the right clothes, or say the right things, they'll let you have a sip. Well, after a few swigs you're sloppy drunk."

Tyler and I both hung our heads.

"One day," she said. "You'll realize, the only people doing valuable things in life, are those who never sipped the Kool-Aid. I want you to be that kind of man. Helpful, kind, and humble."

Tyler mumbled a, "Yes, ma'am." And that was that.

Because he probably wasn't listening, anyway. That's how boys are. But I do hope Tyler understands how lucky he is to be his mother's "special little handsome man." Because the truth is, there is no Tyler.

Tyler is me.

# THE OBSERVER

"Mankind is a damn mess," said ninety-six-year-old Burt, observer of the human condition, and retired auto mechanic. "Just pathetic," observed Burt again. "And that includes you and me, son."

"Burt, you think I'm pathetic?"

"No. Not you, your body."

I touched the roll of tummy hanging over my belt buckle, and reasoned whether it was pathetic, or just a medium-grade of pitiful.

Burt observed again, "It's not your fault, God made you pathetic. Consider how small your heart is. And it never stops. Never. If you were a Chevy Deluxe, you wouldn't last a year."

"What if I was a Nissan Altima?"

"Four months, tops," said Burt, observing Japanese engineering.

"You'll understand when you're older," Burt went on. "Once you get past a certain age, you will see how pathetic you are. It'll start with something small, like back pain. Then, it'll get worse. You'll try things to make it better, you'll convince yourself you've got it licked. And then you'll develop something like arthritis in your feet. Or maybe kidney stones."

I've had a kidney stone before. I had to go to the emergency room. It felt like giving birth to a litter of possums. My doctor kept patting my shoulder, saying, "This too shall pass."

Burt explained. "Then one day, for no reason at all, your back pain will quit working part-time, and switch to full-time. So, eventually, you'll learn to live with it. When you finally adjust, you'll find happiness."

What a relief.

"Until", said Burt. "You fall in the shower and pop your knee. But don't worry, it'll heal. And when it does, you'll develop gout in your big toe."

God help me.

"When the gout goes away you'll want to praise the Lord. Except you can't, because your back has flared up again, and for some unexplainable reason you'll have a yeast infection on your tongue."

"Is that even possible?"

"Yep, your doctor will tell you the infection's nothing to worry about. You'll feel relieved until he mentions that you have diabetes."

"Burt," I interjected. "How can anyone enjoy life if it's so miserable?"

"Who said anything about enjoying life? Life is painful, son, and sad, you can't enjoy life."

"You can't?"

"No, you can only learn to enjoy yourself. If you can do that, nothing in this life can hurt you. Not really."

Well. Maybe he's right.

But kidney stones still hurt like a son of a bitch. And you can quote me on that.

# THE PROCESSIONAL

I remember the police car liked to scare me to death, honking like he did. Lights flashing.

Then, I recall pulling into the ditch on Alabama Highway 41. A string of cars ahead of me did the same thing.

The blue lights rolled by in the empty lane, moving at a turtle's crawl. Close behind: a hearse and a line of vehicles stretching to the horizon.

A woman in a Mazda hopped out to spectate. "I ain't never seen one this big before," she said.

Two young men from a beat up Honda marched toward us. "What is happening?" one of them asked. "Why we stop?" His plates were from Texas, but his Latino accent from further south.

She answered, "Because honey, this is just what we do."

It was the lengthiest procession I have ever seen. One pair of headlights, then another, then another. And another. I counted over one hundred cars, give or take a few. It lasted longer than the Christmas parades from my hometown, which were pitifully small affairs. We had to run the floats around our square twice just to make the whole thing last ten minutes.

While the cars whizzed by, the men from the Honda removed their caps.

The woman from the Mazda remarked, "Have you ever seen so many cars in all your life?"

Then, without warning, one of the young men began to recite a quiet prayer in Spanish. Whatever he said required that he close his eyes. And even though we couldn't understand his words, we shut our eyes, too. When he finished, there was one "amen," one "thank you Lord," and a "gracias Señor."

Because, this is just what we do.

And we'd do the same thing for someone you love.

# GREENSBORO

If you don't know Greensboro, it's a town of about thirty people, a steeple, a few chickens, a barbecue trailer, and one cat named Wampkus.

Wampkus had a special way of looking at me, like he wanted to kill me.

Jamie and I stayed at a nearby bed and breakfast because my wife believes hotels are oversized litter-boxes with poop on the sheets. The couple next door to us was from New Jersey.

At breakfast, we couples could hardly understand each other. Every time my wife spoke, they exchanged confused glances. And since I happen to speak fluent hand gestures, I agreed to serve as translator. But whenever I attempted translation, my wife swatted me and said, "You're mumbling again, dammit."

And so, I'd look at Wampkus, whose expression never changed.

We learned the New Jerseyans were miserable up north. They hated gray skies, cold winters, and crowded suburbs. And even though they didn't say as much, I suspected their Yankee food was objectionable, too. Nothing but stews, raw veggies, and stale pretzels.

The couple's kids are grown, they're lonely, and looking for Southern real estate. "We want a fresh start," said Mister New Jersey. "Where the people're friendly, where we can get assloads of sunshine."

Assloads? Where was this man's mama?

After our meal, Mister New Jersey shook my hand and said, "Howwzit you guys say goodbye down South?"

"See ya'll later?" I offered.

"Nah, I thought it was, 'yawl come back now, you hear'?'"

Jamie scoffed. "Jeezus, no. We don't say that stupid Hollywood stuff."

My wife will not tolerate the notion that all Southerners speak like Forrest Gump's grandmama chawing a wad of peanut butter.

And so, we bid the New Jerseyans farewell. We all got into our cars to leave. I waved goodbye to hateful little Wampkus. He licked himself.

Jamie cupped her hands over her mouth, and without thinking, she hollered, "Y'all drive safe now, you hear?"

Well.

Even Wampkus smiled at that.

# LIBERTY BOWL

I'm about to break my own rule and write about something I swore I never would. Not since Chad Talbot read a five-page essay on Joe Namath in the fifth grade and put the class to sleep.

May God have mercy on my soul.

It was late December. Cold as hell. My mother went into labor during the first quarter of the Liberty Bowl. Bama versus Illinois.

She huffed like a freight train while my father sat on a vinyl chair watching the black and white television. When the doctor came to visit Mother, he too made a beeline toward the TV. Daddy cranked up the volume.

The voice of announcer, Joe Kapp, called a four-yard touchdown, drowning out Mother's panting.

"Touchdown!" Daddy and the doctor yelled in unison. Then, Mother says they did some happy-cussing.

During bowl games, there are two kinds of cussing. Happy-cussing: reserved for touchdowns. And dog-cussing: when fans instruct opposing coaches or referees to eat a substance commonly found in barnyards and

37

cow pastures.

By the third quarter the delivery room was full; two custodians, four doctors, a handful of lab techs, and one maintenance man, each with his back facing Mother.

Illinois scored. A river of dog-cussing followed.

Mother's contractions got worse. "I felt like a washing machine," she said. "Crammed with a bean bag chair—set on spin cycle."

Fourth quarter: Mother was already baying like a coonhound. The doctor asked if she wouldn't mind keeping her voice down.

And then it happened.

As fate would have it, during Bama's winning touchdown, a long-legged, big-toed, redheaded bullfrog entered this world, covered in crimson slime.

My daddy snatched the toad up and brought it near the television set. He tapped the screen. "You see that man, son? That's Bear Bryant, the best coach of all time."

"Yep," said the doctor to the frog. "This was Coach Bryant's very last game tonight. History in the making. Don't you ever forget that."

Well, there's no way the frog ever would forget such a thing. Because his mother tells him this story every year on his birthday.

And when Bama wins tonight, it will be told again.

# MIDNIGHT SPEEDERS

Do not speed at midnight, on a dark country highway in Macon County. That's what I did, and it was an infamous mistake.

The weather was nice, and I was busy testing my truck's aeronautical capabilities. We traveled so fast my front tires lifted from the road, like a 747 disembarking from the runway.

Then I saw blue lights.

The officer was three-foot high and bow-legged. He sauntered toward our vehicle. And even though he was fifteen years my junior, he said, "Evening, son."

"Good evening, officer."

"You know how fast you were going back there, kiddo?"

Before I could open my mouth to discuss my iniquities with Junior, my wife interrupted in a sugary tone, "Could we hurry this up, officer?" She batted her eyelashes. "Please?"

He smiled politely.

The officer inspected my license. Then, he went on to

explain my first step toward salvation was to confess that I was indeed a speeder, along with my other sins, and ask Jesus into my heart. I bowed my head and apologized for stealing a Seventeen magazine in the sixth grade—years before Junior was ever born.

Jamie fluffed her hair. "Please, officer. I think my cousin, here, has learned his lesson."

"Cousin?" the officer asked. "This man is your cousin?"

"I'm your cousin?" I said.

My wife leaned forward and tugged on her blouse. "That's right, he's my cousin..." She tapped my forehead. "And he's one biscuit short of a blue plate special."

"I am?"

She made her lips get pouty. "Can't you let us go, just this once? I know my cousin would be awfully grateful." She touched her chest. "God knows, I would be."

The officer smiled at her, then winked. He agreed to let me off with a warning and a brief lecture. Then he asked my cousin for her phone number.

So she gave him her mother's.

# ON THAT DAY

If you're reading this, I want you to attend my funeral —whenever that tragic day occurs. Please come. I'll pay your travel expenses. It won't hurt my wallet. Hell, I'll be dead.

I promise, it'll be a fan-damn-tastic beach party. Willie Nelson will be there, since he'll outlive us all. Oh sure, Willie charges a lot for this sort of thing, but my wife, Jamie, will work it all out.

Let's see, what else.

Ah yes, I want you to play baseball before the sun goes down. Let Jamie play first base, Willie can be catcher. Make my mother-in-law pitcher. Don't worry, she'll know how. She knows everything, just ask her.

Barbecue. There will be a ton of that, with Jamie's own sauce, which is a three-generation-old secret. I'll miss that stuff. Eat your fill, then force yourself to eat more. That's what I'd do.

At the proper time, I want you to lay me out on a pinelog raft, with flowers. Not fancy ones, but wildflowers from the pastures of my childhood. I'll be wearing Daddy's wristwatch, covered in Mother's quilt. And I'll have my wife's wedding ring in my pocket; I intend on returning it when I see her again.

Then, push me into the surf and light me on fire. Willie can play "Mamas Don't Let Your Babies Grow Up To Be Cowboys," because as it turns out, I never did.

Afterward, resume eating and dancing like idiots. I want you to have so much damned fun you regret it come morning. Because on that day, life won't be about me anymore. In fact, it never was. It was about friends, baseball, dogs, music, fishing, and women who loved you enough to make barbecue sauce. I was just too self-absorbed to notice that.

Bring your own bottle.

That means you, Willie.

# DOG

I know it's ridiculous, but I wish I could buy you a puppy. If you've got one already, how about two? See, I have this ludicrous idea that dogs could put an end to worldwide hatred, and perhaps even eradicate pissy attitudes.

Take my pissy fifth-grade teacher, for instance. If I could've forced her to wrestle a puppy, it might've cured the old battle-ax. Because whenever you wrestle a puppy, you start saying things in a high-pitched voice, like, "He's a good boy. Yes he is."

And that changes you.

There's something about puppy breath, too. I'll bet the smell of it could cure cancer, if scientists ever found a way to bottle it. And puppy bites. Even though they hurt like hell, they're worth more than real estate, or an all-inclusive cruise to Europe.

Well. Maybe not a cruise.

I wish someone would have the good sense to set up a booth on the street corner and sell puppy love. For five bucks a pop, customers could wrestle the bejeezus out of a happy Labrador. There'd be a single-file line winding clear down the street. I'd be in it.

I once had a dog who demanded to wrestle after supper, every night. The old girl was persistent, too. She'd bark and carry on, then pin me down and sentence me to death by licking.

When she became arthritic, she still wanted to rough-house. But she was fragile. I'd let her pin me down and lick the hell out of my face. Then, she'd collapse and fall asleep with her head on my chest.

I don't know why, but she trusted me, even though I'm proud, and self-centered. Those black eyes seemed to understand almost everything there was to know about me.

Then one day, she closed those eyes for good, while I cried mine out.

I hope God likes to wrestle.

# THE WORRIER

You don't want to know what goes through the mind of a worrier. We worry about money, life-threatening illness, rabid kitty cats, and rollerblades.

I'm a worrier. Take, for instance, a harmless ant bite, it looks an awful lot like a black widow bite. So do mosquito bites, raised freckles, and flecks of barbecue sauce.

Once while doing yard work, a small spider darted up the leg of my pants. It made it as far as my you-know-whats. I stripped down to bare flesh, only to discover our neighbor watching me do a version of the Roger Rabbit unfit for cable television.

I worry about more than just spiders. Whenever someone offers me a drink, I sniff the glass for unfamiliar residues. I'm no dummy. I've watched Dateline before. One minute you're making smalltalk, then BAM, a little antifreeze in your Gatorade and you're in the back of a van.

I worry when my gas tank falls below a quarter. That's why, I carry five-gallon gas cans, and a dolly.

45

Some folks carry only gas cans. Fools. One day they'll find themselves in the Sahara, a million miles from a Tom Thumb. Ergo: the dolly.

I'm like you. I worry about carbs, saturated fat, politics, and Christmas lights. Yes, Christmas lights. I saw a news report that claimed decorative lights were responsible for fifty percent of holiday deaths. The other fifty percent were from brown recluses.

You want more worries? I once had a minor stomach pain. I went to the doctor. "Aw," he said. "It's nothing serious."

"But, what if I have an infection from eating a piece of undercooked shrimp at Red Lobster?"

"Red Lobster?"

"Just level with me doc, how will it happen? Cold sweats, then kidney failure? Oh my God, I can't feel my teeth."

He placed his hand on my shoulder. "Look, life's too short to be anxious. Everything will be okay, buddy. Drink this, it'll make your stomach feel better."

"It will?"

Because it smells a hell of a lot like antifreeze.

# THESE WOMEN

Boys, the first thing you should know about a Southern woman, is that she is never awkward.

In this part of the world, social awkwardness is a sin. It's even written in the Bible somewhere. Which is why we find it easy to converse with Southern females.

You know what else a Southern lady does? She eats. Seldom will you find her drinking kale smoothies for supper. Thank Jesus. She was born with an appetite that only banana pudding and Sunday-night Bible study can satisfy.

Moving right along. If you're interested in a Southern girl, you'd better care about family. Because if you don't, she'll tell you to go straight to Hell. Which is probably where you're already headed. In fact, speaking of family, you should call your mother right now. Go on, I'll wait.

Right beneath family is football. Your Southern woman knows how this sport works, thank you very much. If you try to explain an onside kick to her, she'll smile and spray Raid on your popcorn.

While watching football, you'll also learn Southern

belles can cuss. They're good at it. And it's not fair, because they hardly ever practice. My wife, Jamie, once stubbed her toe on a brick. She uttered things that made birds fall out of trees.

Along with cussing, Southern gals love the Bible. They quote Proverbs from time to time. But watch out. If she ever combines cussing with Scripture, you're finished.

My cousin sassed his mother once. My aunt grit her teeth and said, "God sayeth, 'spare the rod and spoil the #@*&$! child.'" My cousin's visitation was closed-casket.

The truth is boys, a Southern woman is a product of generations of potlucks, homecomings, and SEC championships. She is strong, and sweet as honey butter. She dresses to the nines, prepares covered dishes of fried chicken, and arrives early to fellowship. She can fix your messy hair with her own spit, strike up conversation with the village idiot, then have mercy enough to bear his children.

Because a Southern girl is many things.

But she is never awkward.

# GREEN ENVY

"You want to see somebody dog-ass ugly?" said my grandfather. "Go look in the mirror."

"Who, me?" I said.

"You're green-ugly with jealousy. You should see yourself."

Well, it was difficult not be envious. I had a friend who'd become famous overnight. In fact, I can't even tell you who he is because you'd recognize him. Then, I'd turn all ugly again, and I just took a shower.

My friend started out as a rural boy, like me. He wore boots, fed chickens, climbed trees, and made slingshots from old cattle bones. Then, at age twelve he landed a role on television and skyrocketed to stardom. When that happened, I became jealous and thus—according to my grandaddy—uglier than a shaved raccoon's ass.

"Grandaddy," I whined. "I wish I were famous."

"Why? Being famous doesn't cure jealousy, and neither does having money. Jealousy is ugliness, and it'll ruin you."

Either way you cut it, it wasn't fair. My friend was

nice-looking, wealthy, and a star. Rumors claimed his mother bought two Mercedes Benzes. Yes, two. I'd only ever seen a Mercedes once, when a flashy preacher visited our church. We never heard the man's sermon, we were all outside touching his car.

When my friend visited town, his mother brought him over to visit—driving her new Benz. We romped through the pastures like we used to. We threw rocks at the abandoned smokehouse, fished the creek, and even climbed trees.

"You know," my friend remarked while dangling from a branch. "I wish things could go back to how they were before I left."

"What?"

"It's true," he said. "We used to play outside like this every day. I miss it. My life is so busy nowadays, I don't have any time. I'm just jealous, I suppose."

Well, I don't care how covetous my friend was of my ordinary life. There was only one jealous-ugly boy that day.

And it was the fool in my mirror.

# FOOTMEN OF DIXIE

God bless the South, and God bless its waiters and waitresses. Noble footmen of Dixie. There, I said it.

When I worked in a restaurant, I once served a Detroit couple. They were picky. I waited on them hand and foot, doing everything except pedaling a unicycle while juggling Ginsu chainsaws. They tipped me thirty-five cents and a Tootsie Roll. The manager shook his head and said, "Cheap yankees, they never tip."

He was right, God love them.

You know what else northern suburbanites seldom do? They don't sit on porches. My buddy from New Jersey thinks porches are for cigarette smokers. "Jersey houses don't even have front porches," he said.

This unsettles me, because folks like my wife and me are always on porches, even when we happen to live in trailers.

And well, the South has a lot of those, too. You might've seen some before. We're not ashamed of our mobile homes. We think they're sassy displays of ambulatory engineering. Especially my aunt Jessie's old single wide, with its flamingos, and beer-can wind chimes.

Some folks think only stupid people live in trailers. Well, that's ridiculous. We're not stupid, just slow. In fact, it took me ten minutes to write this sentence.

My old Literature professor—a miserable buzzard from Chicago—tongue lashed me for being slow arriving for class. He yelled at me before the entire student alumni, "Don't you know what time class starts?"

"No sir," I said bone-crushingly slow. "You must've gone over that before I was here."

So, he gave me a D.

Now there was a man who despised the South.

Too bad for him, because the best thing about the Land of Cotton is our slowness. We love naps, porch-sitting, and barbecues. Big barbecues with pork butt, baked beans, potato salad, and our drunk aunt Jessie. If you're a northerner, you should come join our fun, you'll love it. We carry on famously. All we ask, is that you help with the dishes.

Don't worry about leaving a tip—God forbid.

But would you mind giving Aunt Jessie a ride home?

# BIBLE BELT

I believe in God. And I'm sorry if that doesn't settle well with you, but, he and I get along fine. In fact, except for the Lottery misunderstanding a few weeks ago, I've never had a problem with him.

In Sunday school, my teacher used to say God was invisible. Which was then followed by speculative questions from nine-year-old philosophers with crippling sugar addictions.

"If God's invisible," asked nine-year-old me. "Why don't people bump into him?"

"Because, sweetie. He's in the sky."

"Do birds fly into him?"

"He lives in outer space."

"How about rockets?"

"God avoids them."

"Do astronauts know God?"

"No. Well, maybe."

"Do you think my daddy will ever buy me a pony?"

Sunday school teachers are equipped to deal with such ethereal-minded questions. It's part of the rigorous training they undergo before earning their beehive hairdos.

But, I'm preaching to the choir. If you grew up in the Bible Belt, you already know God isn't what some folks think he is.

Some think God is Wednesday night fellowships; fried chicken, four kinds of potato salad, and Mother's cheese casserole. My uncle would pray a blessing so long at potlucks, our knees locked up and our blood sugar required treatment by IV bags.

Others think God is Saturday night meetings. Where experienced Southern Baptists stretch the word, "Jesus" into eight syllables.

But where I'm from, God is more than that. He's a tire-change for the elderly. He's two men painting Sister Loretta's house because her husband died. God is well attended funerals. He is a day's-worth of helping move furniture just because you own a truck.

God is a hospital visit. He's a Hospice nurse. He's a handwritten card, hot suppers, and football games. He's an old lady who gives tight hugs, a Mexican immigrant who needs a ride home. He's an animal shelter, Mother's homemade bread, or my wife's bedtime kiss. Sometimes, he's even you.

I believe in God because that's how I was raised. I'm sorry it's not fashionable, but I can't help it, dammit.

And I wouldn't want to.

# THE MODERN WOMAN

I'm going to level with you, I'm glad I'm not a woman. Because I couldn't survive today's society. I don't know how modern girls do it.

There was a time when the only things required of women were knowing how to fry bacon and popping sass-mouthed toddlers.

Not today.

Nowadays, to be a card-carrying female, you'd better be able to do more than Granny. To start with, you must have washboard abs, a blossoming career, a husband from the pages of Men's Fitness Magazine, children dressed in seersucker, and at least one expensive handbag.

And if that doesn't give you a nervous breakdown, the modern woman's household must be breathtaking. Her wardrobe: cute, but sassy. Her daughter must play piano. Her boy must compete in baseball, football, basketball, soccer, track, lacrosse, polo, skeet shooting, and speak fluent Spanish.

Had enough? I'm only getting started. Society also

requires women to be gourmet cooks, preparing everything from Sloppy Joes, to blanquette de veau. And let's talk size. Today's woman is instructed to maintain the lithe weight of a malnourished North Korean underwear model—with washboard abs.

Are your palms are getting sweaty? Mine are.

You know what I wish? I wish we allowed women to be themselves, for Christ's sake, Grecian curves and all. I wish ladies swimwear wasn't made of dental floss, that nineteen-year-olds weren't dictating fashion. I wish women of all shapes loved their bodies.

I wish we taught confidence to young girls, and taught young boys to help them find it.

I wish women took more spa vacations, and less sick days. I wish ladies considered gray hair and wrinkles as trophies, not things to cover up. I wish waist sizes weren't measured in numbers, that thick was the new thin. I wish women were proud to be round, firm, meat-eating knockouts, with real smiles, instead of whatever society says they should be.

And one last thing.

To hell with washboard abs.

# WELCOME TO THE CLUB

Fellas, if you're going to marry a Southern girl, welcome to our club. You're about to have the best years of your once-pathetic, Cheeto-Puff-eating life.

And now, I'd like to talk about a few matters for your nuptial consideration.

Let's get started, shall we?

1: Studies show that most Southern women admit to making their husbands sleep on the sofa sooner or later. It's the way life goes. Who knows why? It might be the way you said, "Pass the biscuits." Your Southern peach didn't care for your snide tone, or the way you held your fork. Thus, you've ruined supper and pissed in the proverbial punch bowl, and now she's locking the door.

2: Once upon a time, you had a closet. Now your wife has four—including the guest bedroom. You're welcome to keep your clothes under the bed where the cat sleeps.

3: Millions of years ago, happy Southern couples watched television programs from start to finish. That's how civilization worked. But around 1492, a bunch of wives got together and invented the DVR so they could pause and rewind. Lineal television-viewing as we knew it vanished. Now, it takes seven days to watch one episode of Dancing With the Stars.

4: Your wife owns a billion shoes. It's her religion. She has a pair of pumps for walking the dog, and another for chopping garlic.

5: When your wife says, "I don't care what we eat tonight," beware. Studies show that low blood sugar has transformed her Southern brain into a suitcase bomb. I hate to break it to you. Your Dixie butterbean is exhibiting early symptoms of I'm-about-to-whip-your-ass-zheimers.

6: If you ever hear your magnolia blossom use words like, "We need to talk," she's about to back over you with the truck.

7: Your house always smells funny. No, it's not the dog, it's you. In fact, if it weren't for your venison-like odor, the Yankee Candle company would go belly-up.

8: Never use the word, "period." Not even when you're talking about English grammar.

9: United States Congress ruled it a federal offense for men to tamper with residential thermostats in forty-nine states. Only women and their mothers inherit this privilege. Thousands of males undergo public execution for flaunting this statute. In some foreign countries, like California, castration.

10: If you ask your honeypot "what's wrong," and she grudgingly replies, "nothing," I have good news. New evidence suggests there is indeed nothing wrong with your Southern wife, but that you're a greasy prick for forgetting to take out the recycle bin.

You know the drill.

Hit the sofa, pal.

# TO MY UNBORN CHILD

To the unborn son I've never had, and never will:

I wish I could watch you play baseball. Especially when you're a teenager. You'd be hell on the field, I just know it. Though your old man was an awful first baseman, he truly loves the game. Which, as it happens, is a lot like life.

But teenagers don't know biscuits about life, and that goes double for you. I don't mean to sound degrading because I'll bet you're a pretty smart kid. I'm only saying it because adults don't know much either. Take, for instance, this adult.

Don't be ashamed of what you don't know. You're young, enjoy your naivety. You only get it once.

Another thing: do yourself a favor, avoid folks who don't know where they're going. People with dead smiles; who couldn't cry if they wanted. They're blind, and they'll poke your eyes out if you're not careful. Also, be wary of folks who enjoy praising themselves. They do it because they're scared.

Don't be scared.

I hope you like humility and hate the limelight. At parties, I want you to sit at the kids' table, even when you're in your mid-forties. Don't talk about yourself, talk about others.

Always offer to help with the dishes.

The truth is, son, I don't know a thing about life. But I do know that neither happiness, nor wealth, nor health are worth a damn compared to love. After all, no one can have all three. But you can always have love. In fact, sometimes that's all you'll have.

I'm talking about love that involves a girl who's not afraid to call you a horse's ass. Who eats pulled pork sandwiches on your tailgate because you can't afford football tickets. Who cries easily and doesn't mind seeing you cry. Everyone deserves that kind of love.

Even though I'll never know you, I hope God sends your spirit to a happy family. One who believes in baseball.

And love.

I'm sorry it couldn't be ours.

# ELLIE

You're not going to believe this, but I have a dog in my bed as I write this. A full-grown, hundred-pound, paws the size of pumpkins, loud snoring, number-two-eating coonhound. Her name is Ellie Mae, and her hindparts are on my pillow.

I don't know when this behavior began, but it's unjust and I won't stand for it. I'm an American, for crying out loud. I pay my taxes like everyone else.

When Jamie and I first welcomed Ellie into our home, I made one ceremonious law. And I quote: "No canine abiding within this domicile shall besmirch or slumber upon my bed." I said it in King James English to make it more official. Ellie swore on the Oxford Dictionary she would only wallow in backyards or piles of particularly exotic smelling excrement. She lied.

But before you take Ellie's side, you should know she already has privileges.

For example: Ellie Mae eats better than most Iraqi oil princes. Her daily feasts make my TV dinners look like Army rations. She eats Lamb and rice for breakfast—I'm not making this up—we prepare actual lamb. For lunch: crockpot beef and potatoes. Mid-afternoon snack: toilet paper. For supper: a bacon cheeseburger, chili cheese fries, and an ice cold Budweiser.

That's not all, Ellie also owns real estate. You heard me right. In 2009, we began construction on Ellie's one-bedroom, no bath, colonial revival cottage in our backyard. She doesn't even use it, she rents it to a family of squirrels who keep late hours and blast loud rock music.

And now she's laying smack-dab on my mattress.

You should hear this animal snore. It sounds exactly like she's just eaten a whole Birkenstock. She has the gall to carry on like she owns the place. As if our entire household revolves around her wide-mouthed grin and skillet-sized paws. Well, I'm not going to tolerate it. I don't give a cuss how cute she is. This is my house, dammit. And I don't have time for this, I've got more important things to be doing today.

Like cooking ten pounds of lamb.

# MOTHER-IN-LAW

I'm sorry if this is offensive, because I consider myself a sincere gentleman. I mean it. I open doors for ladies, watch my language, and read comic books. But the truth is—and I can hardly say it—my mother-in-law just saw me naked.

Don't make me repeat myself.

It happened just a few minutes ago, right in my own house, and I'm traumatized. I've got a lot of unpleasant feelings swimming inside me at the moment. Some of which date back to middle-school gym showers.

The truth is, I can't explain how it happened. All I know is: one moment I'm waltzing across my empty house, enjoying the invigorating January air. Then WAM, a peeping-thomasina is in my kitchen.

"Miss Mary!" I squealed—but in a masculine tone. "How'd you get in here?"

"I have a key, ding-a-ling."

"Please don't use that word."

She handed me a stack of envelopes. "I brought your mail."

And since I have a knack for saying intelligent things, I answered, "But Miss Mary, I'm naked."

She agreed.

Without uttering another word, I trotted to the bedroom. One hand covering my unmentionables, the other shielding the region where the Good Lord split me.

The thing is, a man's house is his sanctuary. Mother-in-laws can't just pop in for half-price peepshows whenever the mood strikes. There are laws against this sort of thing.

In some countries, they would've already deported her. She's lucky we live in America, or she'd be assembling jack-in-the-boxes in a sweat shop. Because Canadians have zero-tolerance policies on nudity crimes.

I suppose I don't know what happens now that Mary has seen the real me. What will the holidays be like? Say, Thanksgiving with the family? Who prays the blessing? It can't be me, and it sure as hell can't be her.

Isn't it sad how something like an innocent pair of white hindcheeks can rip a family apart? I'd like to know where two traumatized people go from here.

Mary suggested we go for drinks and dinner.

# DIE

Kill me now. My wife has put us on a diet.

It all started when she tried on her high-school jeans —against my strong advice. She discovered the jeans were barely big enough for Maui Barbie, so she punched the refrigerator hard enough to dent it.

Her first move was outlawing my Twinkies and Butterfingers. Then, she prepared baked tofu and kale salad doused in white vinegar. Vinegar, as you know, is intended for stripping paint off old swing sets, not for salads.

Allow me to list some other entrees. Most of which, you'll notice, are not Butterfingers.

Brown rice and lima beans. Spinach greens with a side of jack squat. Cabbage water soup—which tastes like a septic tank. Artificial meatloaf; made from oatmeal, vegetable broth, and a baseball mitt.

Shoot me in the armpit.

Of course, the hardest things are the mood swings. To protect the innocent, I won't tell you which of us suffers psychopathic episodes, but I will say that it's Jamie. Last night, when a commercial advertised Jimmy Dean sausage, she put another dent in our refrigerator.

To make matters worse, Jamie pre-packages lunches to suppress my hankerings for Butterfingers. Today's gratifying banquet: celery dipped in what looks like Vaseline. Tomorrow: lawn clippings. The day after that: radishes.

I don't even know why supermarkets sell radishes. I've never seen anyone in the checkout aisle buying radishes with their roast chicken and Budweiser. If you've never had a radish, they taste like pine knots soaked in bleach.

I'll be frank with you, mankind is not meant to eat radishes, nor diet. It's no coincidence the first three letters of "diet," are what they are. I can spell.

My wife is trying to kill me and it's working. Calorie-cutting is making me weak, I can't even use the toilet without getting winded. I feel like I could sleep two years after the lunch I just ate.

Which as it happens, consisted of exactly one ugly red radish.

And six Butterfingers.

# CELLPHONES

I can quit any time I choose, dammit. I'm not addicted. I can stop playing with my phone whenever I please. In fact, I'm putting it down right now—after I check my email.

Okay, I'm setting it down for real this time.

Just one second.

Anyway, the thing is, I like smartphones. They've made me into the vegetable I am. I used to be a boring idiot. But now, I'm a boring idiot who can't make eye-contact. My wife notices my minor problem. For instance: when eating supper, I often play Fruit Ninja while she explains exactly how she'll divorce me if I don't put down my phone.

To which I'll respond, "No, sweetie, those pants don't make your butt look big." Which is a foolproof response for fake-listeners all over the world.

But don't let my wife deceive you, she's no iPhone-saint either. Last night, Jamie spent six hours staring at her phone. That's almost an entire workday's worth of using her thumbs. While she played Candy Crush, I scrolled Facebook asking things like, "Honey, do I look as old and wrinkled as my high-school girlfriend?"

"No, dear," Jamie answered. "Those jeans don't make your butt look big."

Yes, I know. Smartphones have supposedly destroyed interpersonal communication, handicapping American teenagers, paralyzing procreation amongst sea turtles. Blah blah blah, horse hockey. I don't even want to remember what I did at stoplights before my iPhone, much less what I did while driving at high speeds, or mowing the lawn.

I'm just kidding. I don't mow lawns.

I use my phone so often—and I'm not making this up —I've developed sprained thumbs. The doctor said there's an official name for this pandemic sweeping the nation. It's called: sprained thumbs. He recommends I find other hobbies besides Netflix, and shut down the phone so my thumbs can rest.

"Doc," I said. "Please tell me you don't mean I'm supposed to power down my phone for good."

"No, son," he said. "Those pants don't make your butt look big."

# ABOUT A GIRL

You would've liked her—everyone did. She had soot-black hair that hung down to her lower back. If I close my eyes, I can still see that hair. Because boys, you see, love long hair.

Don't believe any who say otherwise.

I was miles beneath her—along with four million other freckle-faced toads. We all vied for her attention and never got more than a smile. Though a smile was good enough. Those were simpler times.

She was going to be a doctor, a lawyer, or a teacher. There aren't exactly many choices in a small town. She was smart as the guts of a calculator, and pure hell on the volleyball court. Basketball too.

I only heard her sing once, at a wedding. "Savior Like a Shepherd Lead Thee." She had the ability to make men weep like willows, and young boys sob like men.

And then she fell apart.

Folks used the C-word, said it was a mass on her brain. But most said things like, "It's a damn shame about that girl." And it was, too.

Her friends packed her room so full of flowers the greenery threatened to burst her windows. And she had more Hallmark stationary than a drugstore aisle of greeting cards.

On the day she died, her mother was beside her. She swears a cold wind blew through the room.

"It was like someone left a window open," her mother said. "And then her eyes went out like lightbulbs. At the funeral, the preacher told everyone she had 'gone with the wind.' I liked that."

I'll bet.

"But," her mother went on, "She didn't die that day, it happened long earlier. She died the morning the nurses shaved head. Oh, it killed us all. Her hair was her favorite thing about herself. And this world took it from her."

Well, I don't know a thing about life, and I don't know where her soul went off to. The same place we all go I guess.

But wherever she is, I know she's got her hair.

# HAPPY CAMPERS

In the summer of 2004, we set out to camp across the great American South in a nylon tent about the size of a residential bathtub.

Bound for Chattanooga we shot out of town with coolers, every blouse my wife owned, and our cat, Rascal. When I protested that Rascal didn't belong on our camping trip; my wife suggested I eat a cow patty.

So, Rascal spent the entire ride coiled around my neck like an orthopedic brace. And somewhere around Georgiana, she managed to nick my eyeball with her back claws. Yes.

My eyeball.

Our first night camping in Greenville wasn't bad—from what I saw with my good eye.

The second night, we pulled in to Oak Mountain Park. After scouting for the perfect spot, I finally pitched our tent on hallowed brown-recluse mating grounds. Rascal licked herself with earnest while spiders big enough to file for health insurance procreated on our floor.

The next morning, after tossing our spider-infested tent into the dumpster, we drove to Noccalula Falls Park. It was magnificent. If you've never been to Noccalula — pronounced Nqwxvzkllrygha—it's worth a visit. There are rock formations, gardens, trails, and lots of other places for getting into heated public arguments with your spouse.

That night, without a tent, we slept beneath the humid summer sky in our sleeping bags. Rascal nestled herself in my armpit while I watched strange clouds gather above us, blotting out the moon. And then, all hell broke loose. North Alabama received a record-breaking rainfall, tipping the scales at some seven million inches.

The next night was Mentone, Alabama. It was still raining. We slept in the truck. Rascal puked on my lap. Jamie snored.

The following morning: we limped into Chattanooga, where I vowed to never tent camp again. I checked in to the Holiday Inn. I could've kissed the lady behind the counter. The hotel was spectacular. Hot showers, cable television. We ate so many Cheetos my eyepatch turned orange. I left Rascal to sleep in the front seat of my truck.

Well.

I didn't know cats could pee so much.

# BOYS

Boys. Help the girls. It's in the rule book.

Even though you'll find many females are strong enough to take care of themselves, help them. Every one. Old and young. Even the girl who's unusually tall for her age, who sits behind you in class, who pins you down on the playground and assaults you with a library book.

She does it because she likes you.

Carry heavy things for her, open doors, walk with her, make conversation.

My uncle once explained, "Being a gentleman is just a fancy way of admitting you idolize women and worship their mothers."

And fellas, there's nothing wrong with that.

Get messy. You don't need me to tell you that. But even so, there are smartphones and video games out there that beg for your attention. I hope you don't forget log forts in the woods, or red capes, or leaping off doghouses like Superman—thereby fracturing your ulnar in three places. Because when you're older, you'll wish you'd done those things.

Do yourself a favor and ignore peer pressure. If you don't know what that is, don't worry. Remember: whenever some unfortunate clown says something like, "Aw, you big wimp," just roll your eyes. Then respond with, "I zigs and zags, I to's and fro's. That's what you ask me, that's what you knows. Don't worry 'bout me, I can take care of myself."

Your friend will say, "Huh?"

Then you'll say, "The Br'er Rabbit said that."

If your friend doesn't know who you're speaking of, find a new friend.

Listen to people. Especially to those less fortunate than you. Don't give advice, dammit. People don't need it, and you don't have any. And neither do I. Just listen. Listen to a girl when she tells you what's bothering her. Act as though she's quoting scripture.

And if you should ever find you're having a hard time listening, then offer to help her do something.

Because boys help girls.

It's in the rule book.

# SMALL TOWNS

I don't care what people say about small towns. Yes, they may be small—and a little behind—but they're the only places remaining where kids still ride bikes in the streets. Where teachers still refer to students by their older siblings' names.

In small communities, things are greater than they seem. For instance, church is not just a Sunday thing. Church is bunco club, bridge club, Rotary Club, Kiwanis, AA meetings, Wednesday potlucks, banana pudding, and Vacation Bible School.

If you're visiting from a bigger city, you won't find seven-dollar espresso drinks anywhere in town. In fact, the only place to buy anything like that is the gas station up the road. And we're sorry there aren't any croissants to go with your piss-warm coffee. But a few miles back, you can try the new Walmart. That thing is like Disney World theme park—only with less teeth.

No matter which town you visit, you'll find a cafe

where men eat breakfast and talk about Cam Newton. Or about when Nick Saban converted bottled water into Cabernet Sauvignon.

You'll also catch up on some bone-crushing gossip while you're at the Piggly Wiggly. You might even hear some fresh dirt about yourself. But don't worry, none of it's true. Your critics got bored and started making things up. Folks can be cruel as the grave when they want to be. How do you think I got the nickname Critter? You don't want to know, and neither did that poor possum.

But there's something else you'll find in theses places. Something you won't find in the suburbs.

To understand what I'm talking about, try this: attend a local funeral. Do you see all those people lining up back to the curb? They're all waiting to shake a young widow's hand and say something like, "If there's anything I can do, ma'am, just call." And they mean it, dammit. They'll prove it with nearly fifty thousand covered casseroles.

You'll see that kind of thing a lot around here. Call it whatever you want.

We call it love.

And it gets harder to find the further away you go.

# HOW TO SAY GRACE

If you're going to be a dignified Southerner, you're going to need to learn to say grace like one. You can tell a lot about a person by the way they ask the blessing. That's because there are more wrong ways than right ones in this part of the world.

For example: poems and rhymes are quite improper here. I learned this the hard way. "Oh God," said childhood-me. "Bless this food, before us set, it needs all the help that it can get. Amen—and awomen."

That's how I lost my left molar.

Then there's the ever-famous:

> *"Thank you God for my hands and mouth,*
> *For cathead biscuits from the South.*
> *For lukewarm bourbon in a glass,*
> *Uh oh, here comes mama to slap my..."*

Well, you get the idea.

It's also exponentially rude to use King-James English when praying. "Almighty, we beseech thee," recited our pimple-faced youth pastor. "Lord, verily doth thy visage beam, yea, upon us from thither shall we lift thine eyes..." blah blah blah. Whatever.

Bring on the fried chicken.

Don't make longwinded monologues. That's a rookie mistake, too. My cousin—I won't use his real name—Rickie Dickie Smithandwesson III, takes pride in long blessings. When we stand around the supper table, Rickie Dickie recites the entire Old Testament backward. Before he ever says Amen, three elderly aunts' knees lock up, and two uncles suffer diabetic comas.

The truth is, God doesn't need long prayers. In fact, God doesn't need to hear anything, he already knows what you need before you ask. Just make sure you don't pray like a smart-ass. Take me, for instance, I am a smart-ass.

Just last night I prayed:

> *"Oh gracious Father,*
> *My heart is stabbed with riot.*
> *Please save me from my wife,*
> *She's got me on a diet."*

My wife followed my benediction with:

> *"Oh Lord, to Thee I come with great remorse,*
> *Please forgive us our divorce,*
> *Forgive my husband, who must be sick.*
> *He's a low-down, dirty, greasy prick."*

And all God's people said:
Awomen.

# A FINE OLD GIRL

God made no better creature than a Labrador retriever. I've owned six in my lifetime. The rest were mutts and coonhounds—not counting Pete the goldfish. They were all good animals. But none like Cody.

Cody was my childhood chocolate Labrador—and my sister. She had yellow eyes and a soft demeanor. Each night, she slept at the foot of my bed and snored loud enough to wake Moses. I'd grown accustomed to fussing at her, mumbling things in a half-awake voice. "Cody-quit-it," I'd moan. "I-say-quit-it-now."

And then I'd throw a pillow to show I meant business.

Cody spent most of her life outdoors. She was the only dog I ever had who followed me wherever I went. If I walked three miles, she walked three—which was how far it was to the river. If I stopped hiking, she stopped. I fished, she waited. I swam, so did she.

More than that, Cody was the luckiest damn dog alive. And that's no exaggeration. The old girl cheated death more times than a jackrabbit. She'd fallen through ice, taken buckshot to the hip, and was even hit by a tractor.

Cattle farms next to ours wouldn't tolerate Cody hopping fences to visit the cows. So, the ranchers set out bowls of food laced with rat killer. Cody, who never turned down free lunches, survived such poisoning on three occasions.

Then, there was the copperhead that leapt off its belly and popped her right on the lip. Cody laid still for a whole week while I cried, promising God I'd read my Bible and quit cussing. It was a miracle when Cody finally recovered. The next morning, I enrolled in Sunday school class and I never uttered another swear word again.

The old girl liked to sleep. I've never seen a dog slumber so hard. Of course, all that swimming, running, and eating is enough to make any creature dog-tired. Even a Labrador. The truth is, I miss her laying by my feet, and that orange collar. I miss her filthy odor.

Just last night, I awoke in a sleepy-fog and mumbled, "Quit-snoring-Cody, I-say-quit-it-now."

But it was only a dream.

Because Cody quit snoring a long time ago.

# NO PLACE FOR A BOY

A funeral parlor is no place for a thirteen-year-old boy. They don't belong there. They belong outside, carrying a rifle, hunting dove. They should be riding bikes, throwing rocks at abandoned rusty Buicks in overgrown fields. A boy should not be near a casket, shaking hands with men who look as awkward in their neckties as he does.

Because after three hundred handshakes, a boy starts to get tendonitis of the elbow, and he slurs his words. His knees lock up and he loses the ability to think.

I saw one such boy. He was fading, getting hungry. I got to the funeral parlor late, wearing a necktie fit for a monkey, just like him. He stood by his mother, with a flat look on his face.

It's a look that is neither happy nor sad. Neither hot nor cold. Not grim, nor concerned. It's the basic look of being alive. Because that's all that boy was. One big numb pile of human-being.

By the time I made it to him, the boy had already heard the top fifty phrases of the day. They all sound the same and they get stuck in your head.

Trite one-liners like: "Your daddy's in a better place, boy." Or, "He's at peace now." Or my personal favorite, "Be strong for your mama."

I shook the boy's hand and didn't say a word. Because he wouldn't have remembered a damn thing I said, anyway. I'm not even kin to him. But I've thought a lot about it, and if I could've told him something, I would've said these words:

> *My friend, I wish I could stand in your place,*
> *Today, and the for next thirty years,*
> *Because, you see, I've worn your face,*
> *I'm not as old as I appear.*
>
> *But God won't let me do that for you,*
> *And you really wouldn't want Him to,*
> *For after thirty years, you'll grow strong,*
> *Somehow you'll learn to carry on.*
>
> *And when you're done growing,*
> *You'll be the one who writes this poem.*

Like I've just done for you.

# OLD TIME RELIGION

Yes, we believe in God. We know it's not fashionable, and that you think we're wackos. But we're not apologizing.

Why should we?

The southeast section of America touts the most religious states in the Union. And I didn't make that up, I heard it on the country radio station, right after hearing, "Clinging to an Unchanging Hand'"—Conway Twitty's gospel masterpiece.

We flat-out like the idea of God. And we can't quit liking this idea because you think we're Southern-fried wing-nuts. Religion is in our drinking water.

Case and point: once, outside Tuscaloosa, I saw two fellas in a parking lot about to fight—I'm not making this up. The troublemaker raised his fists and shouted, "God's 'bout to give me victory!"

The other man, nearly nine-feet tall, shed his Lynyrd Skynard jacket and said. "I'm fixin' to make a River of Life flow out of you, son."

I bet ten bucks on Lynyrd.

Before either of the God-fearing cage-fighters took a swing, a teenager butted between them. The boy began reciting the Sermon on the Mount in a loud voice, with trembling hands. In that moment, we all set our beers down and bowed our heads.

Which is what our mama's taught us to do when someone quotes Jesus.

The two hoodlums never threw a single blow; four onlookers came forward for salvation; I lost ten damn dollars.

Our religion gets bad press, and I'm offended by that. Because I'm Southern Baptist—most of the time.

Sociopathic Bible-thumpers have lifted their legs and tee-teed on what we believe, waving their ridiculous hand-painted signs outside courthouses. Whoever these angry folks work for, it sure ain't God.

I know this, because I know God, we were college roommates for eight years—and no, I'm not a doctor, just bad at math.

See, I like how God makes camellia's bloom, and oak trees grow lopsided. I enjoy good rains, and summer days with enough sunshine to melt earwax. I like dandelions, puppies, babies, and art.

> *I like Coca-Cola, peanuts, and Conway Twitty.*
> *Montgomery, Alabama, and Oklahoma City.*
> *Touchdowns, Cam Newton, and baseball gloves.*
> *And I like God.*
> *Because God is love.*

# A NIGHT IN SOUTH GEORGIA

It was seven at night, the middle of April, a two-lane highway. On the radio: Glen Campbell's "Gentle On My Mind" played while I nodded off behind the wheel. I don't remember how exactly it happened, but it did.

Then, a loud boom.

It sounded like a baseball bat smashed the hood of my truck. The last sight I recalled was a tree limb stabbing through the windshield.

The man who found me was enormous. He wore camouflage with an orange cap. He helped me into his big vehicle. Then he said, "Tell me your name, son."

All I could answer was, "G-G-Glen Campbell."

His single-wide was located deep within the thicket of South Georgia. His wife fed me pot roast, potatoes, and carrots. Their nine-year-old daughter asked questions like, "Why is there a black spot on your forehead?"

To which I answered, "It's not black, it's purple."

I showered in their mud room. I wore borrowed pajama's, ten sizes too big, and slept in their spare bed.

The next morning, they fed me sausage and hash browns until I was sick.

At the table, the nine-year-old asked, "Are you married?"

"No."

"Do you want to get married?"

"Someday, I suppose."

"To me?"

"Is that a proposal?"

She wrinkled her nose. "What's that?"

"It's when a boy asks a girl, 'Will you marry me?'"

"Of course I'll marry you, but I'll tell you upfront, I'm hyphenating my last name."

When my cousin arrived to pick me up, the man's wife handed me a plate of cookies. She said, "I'm glad Phillip found you when he did, or else you'd have been out there all night, nobody comes down these roads."

"You know," she went on. "He actually thought you might be an angel."

"Me?" That was the pot calling the kettle purple.

She nodded. "Phillip thinks God sends people to test us. To see if we put others first."

Well.

I'm about as far from being an angel as one can get without carrying a pitchfork. Real angels, you see, aren't like me. They're strong, kind, selfless.

Some are invisible.

Others go by the name Phillip.

# HERE COMES THE SUN

Gray weather feels a lot like taking a field trip to Hell. Whenever the sky gets like this, I sit by a windowsill unable to gather enough energy for basic tasks; like folding clothes, cutting grass, bathing the cat, or eating barbecue ribs.

I start to miss the sun, the same way I might miss trees, grass, or ice cream if they vanished behind clouds.

Or dirt, especially the red kind. Or muddy creeks and rivers, or large mouth bass and catfish. Or sausages from Conecuh County, biscuits made by hand, pork butts, pork shoulders, and barbecued ribs.

As it happens, I hold a longstanding county-fair record for eating the most consecutive ribs without suffering thrombosis. I'll show you my trophy sometime —if ever these God-forsaken clouds go away.

Kids. If clouds covered all the kids up, I'd miss them. And babies, too. Fat ones that wiggle when they laugh, like flopping trout. I love children. They remind me of who I am inside—a tall kid with a mortgage.

And since I'm giving my big fat opinions, here's

another: I wish pop-singers would quit dressing like sex-toys. Don't they know kids watch them on television? Don't they know there's more to life than sex? Do they even know what music is?

I guess not.

Well I'll tell you what real music is. Go visit a classroom full of five-year-olds singing, "Zachaeus Was A Wee Little Man." Or: "This Little Light Of Mine." You'll hear all the real music you can stand.

I've never smiled as big as I did when I taught Sunday school, watching twenty kids shatter lightbulbs using only their voices.

We used to sing like that, you and I.

I'm glad we were children once, before the clouds of adulthood came. Because in those days, we were naive enough to be singers, fingerpainters, and storytellers with small vocabularies.

I wish we had small hands and stinky feet again. I wish we were curious and too distracted to be sad. I wish we laughed so hard we peed ourselves, and that we gave lots of hugs like we used to.

And God, if you can hear me:

I wish I had some more barbecue ribs.

# MY VALENTINE

I've seen her climb a mountain. On her birthday. No joke. I was beside her, praying for God to kill me. When we made it back to earth, she was so overcome with emotion all she could say was, "Sumbitch."

To which I agreed, "Sumbitch."

And then we cried.

I won't forget the time she landed in the emergency room, her tooth half knocked out. The doctor said, "We're going to give you a shot in the gums ma'am. And it's gonna hurt like fire."

She nearly broke my hand, and screamed, "Sumbitch!"

The nurses thought she was going to pass out.

But then, her husband yelled, "Sumbitch!" and fell out like a Pentecostal.

And years later, I saw her collapse on the floor when a nurse broke the news that her own father had died. She cried so much, the snot and tears almost ruined her shirt. And her husband's.

I saw her mind go numb on the day of his visitation. I watched her change into a full-woman when they closed the casket.

It must've aged her twenty years inside. Though you'd never know it on her face.

God, she hates those fine lines around her eyes. But not me. She's earned them, dammit, and I like them. They make her look like a real human being. Someone who knows things. Genuine things.

And sometimes late at night, I think about how brief all things are. And then I feel sad to think that one day I won't be here to tease her, or scrub her back. All women need someone to tease them and scrub their backs.

It makes me sorry to imagine the morning one of us sips our coffee alone. When one of us slams our thumb in the cabinet and yells, "sumbitch," in solitary. And no one says it back.

You see, I know life's not fair; that someday, time will select one of us to fall. That one will miss the other so much they'll quit eating, sleeping, and even crying. And I can only thank the Good Lord above.

That it's not today.

Happy Valentine's Day, Jamie

# IF I WERE RICH

If I were rich, and I mean filthy rich, I'd buy a dog shelter first. Hands down, no questions. It would be a gigantic farm, big enough to house hundreds—no thousands of dogs.

They would be free to roam, drinking out of a huge sculptured toilet out back. I'd call our ranch, "Dog Gone It," or, "Our Dog is an Awesome Dog." Anyway, you get the idea.

The second thing I'll do is gather the county's unfortunate kids and offer them rooms and food. They can take care of our dogs; groom them, read them Dr. Seuss books. And our children are free to live on the farm until retirement age. At which point we'll transfer them to the Dog Works in Mysterious Ways nursing home.

You'll find a school on our property, one with doggie doors. While Miss Roberts teaches the underprivileged multiplication, Otis and Sadie bound into the classroom —tennis balls in mouths.

Miss Roberts will hate me for that.

Our farm holds weekly food-raisers for the hungry. Notice, I didn't say FUND-raisers. No sir. This isn't a place rich folks promenade new dresses, or take selfies with celebrities. Or where philanthropists are glorified in magazines, sipping champagne, making conversations that are about as shallow as a pile of spit. To hell with their narcissism.

I won't have it.

Here at Dog Bless You Farms, we don't care about impressing you. We care about fun. And movies.

Every Friday is movie night. We show old black and white films, and early Disney movies, like Lady and the Tramp. Admission is free. You can bring a blanket and picnic if you like. Come meet the children who live here —adopt one if you can. If you can't, then befriend one.

And I hope you like dogs, because we have millions of them, and they love movie night. Almost as much as they like your bucket of fried chicken.

If you happen to enjoy the farm, and you'd like to donate money to our cause; don't.

Go start your own.

# SICK

I'm sick. Dog sick. I woke up yesterday with a throat that felt like I tried to swallow a brick. I tried to get out of bed, but couldn't. So, I rolled onto my back and summoned my wife by ringing a little bell.

She loves that.

The first thing you should know about me is that I'm a real man—if I haven't disclosed that already. And men are not good at being sick. This is because we grew up with a mama whose sole occupation in life was to:

1. make grilled cheeses.

2. rub our tummies.

Women make good mothers because, it's a proven fact, they're experts in the field of sickness. Take my wife, Jamie, for instance, she's a professional sick person. Whenever she's ill, she sports pajamas, watches movies, reads books, plays crosswords, pays bills, writes thank-you cards, recaulks the bathroom, and paints the den.

Whenever I'm sick, I lay on my stomach without pants, and ring my bell.

Look, we men become depressed when we're sick. It's biological. Most days, we work harder than Forty-Mule-Team Borax, doing strenuous activities like watching ESPN Draftpicks. But now, due to crippling fatigue and moderate sinus pressure; I need a grilled cheese.

Remember, don't use cheddar, my mama makes hers with American. Also, sweetie, if you're going to the store, could you pick up some chips? I'm feeling weak. Just ringing this little bell makes me lightheaded.

Have you seen the remote?

I'm out of Gatorade.

Ladies, don't resent us for being like this. You'd be this way too if your mothers spoiled you like ours did. Our mama's rolled the televisions into our bedrooms, spoon fed us, then took our temperatures with thermometers designed for Shetland ponies—and I don't mean under the tongue. Whenever we rang our little bells, mama brought grilled cheeses cut into quarters, garnished with potato chips, and all the ginger ale we could stand.

So go easy on us. Put yourselves in our shoes. Imagine how life-anguishing it would be if your wife forgot to cut your damn sandwich.

Then smashed your bell with a hammer.

# ALL THE GOOD

There are two things you should know about me: (a) I shower twice a day, and (b) I never pick up hitchhikers.

Thus, when I saw a shaggy boy using his thumb—a tactic often used by serial killers—I surprised myself. I broke my own rule and pulled over.

His name is Ethan. He's hitchhiking across the southern U.S. to Texas. "It's kind of an experiment," said the innocuous ball of facial hair. "To see if folks are nice enough to help a complete stranger."

"But, don't you think hitchhiking is dangerous?"

"Nah, I believe humans are good."

The fact is, despite mankind's flaws, I'm inclined to agree with my smelly-ass friend. Only, I don't need to swear off showering prove it.

You want kindness? I once watched a woman coax a confused dog from the middle of a four-lane highway. The stray mutt was half-blind with cataracts. When it was over, I'm not sure which of them was more grateful to be alive.

How about this: in my aunt's neighborhood, three

teenagers mow an old man's lawn once a week. No charge. They've been doing it since his hip surgery five years ago. And as I understand, they still do. Except, they're college-age now.

Then, there's the time I met an elderly man who lived in a tent. He and his son camped behind the Catholic church. "I'm the pope," the man said, "I always sleep near my blessed chapels."

The man's son was older than me, he explained, "Pardon my dad, he's senile. If I didn't stay with him, there's no telling what would happen." He smiled a gap-toothed grin "I love my dad."

There's no doubt about that, friend.

You can say what you want about the state of humankind. And God knows, you have a right to think the worst of us. Because we're selfish animals, and several of us could stand some grooming—namely, Ethan.

But I believe something good lives in people. Something transcending common evil. Others believe it stronger than I do. And they're willing to bet their thumbs on it.

I hope young Ethan finds whatever he's after.

Say, for instance, a shower.

# HOW TO BE MARRIED

Whatever you once thought about marriage, forget it. People have matrimony all wrong. It's not about chapels, bouquets, or grooms' cakes with deer antlers. Marriage is about vowing before God that you will hereby spend three quarters of your life painstakingly fussing about what's for supper.

Look son, I know you think you're marrying a girl. You're not. What you're really getting is someone with low blood sugar, unable to decide between butterbeans and Olive Garden.

It will go like this: the moment you awake, your wife rolls over, blowing her stink-breath into your innocent young face. "What do you want for supper tonight, dear?" she asks, like Scarlett O'Hara, who's just polished off a can of oysters.

"How should I know?" you might say. "I just woke up." Then, you roll onto your other side. There, your dog stares at you with even worse breath, saying, "Did you decide on supper yet, dork?"

The answer is no. It's always no.

Besides, your wife only wants to hear your suggestions so she can answer, "Aw, I don't want pizza, we just ate that last February." And by that time, your moderate disagreement will mushroom into a full-blown discussion.

Which raises another issue. Married people don't fight, we conduct "discussions." This is especially true when one of us is about to get his teeth knocked in.

Also, during such "discussions," you must never admit you're "angry." That's not how married people talk. Explain instead that you're "frustrated," or perhaps, "unsettled." Take Jamie, for instance, she hasn't been angry in fifteen years. Not even when I backed the truck into the garage. Which unsettled the unholy piss out of her.

Also, within your repartee, refrain from using words like, "always," or, "never." Marriagewise, we refer to these as negative absolutes, and they will ALWAYS get your throat slit by a can opener.

A sample sentence not to use: "Jeezus, Jamie, why do you ALWAYS buy me the wrong kind of beer?" This should be retranslated into, "Can I come back inside now, it's cold out here?"

To which her answer will be: no.

Not until you decide what we're having for supper.

# SOUTHERN DRAWL

I don't want to alarm you; but Southern accents are disappearing. The Associated Press reported that "Due to an influx of new residents within the lower U.S., Dixie dialects are fading into oblivion."

Oblivion.

Well, my cow in the morning—as Jimbo's mother would say. I don't even know where Oblivion is. Somewhere up near Cincinnati, I think. This will never do.

If we lose Southern drawls, that means there will be no more rednecks. And if there are no more rednecks wandering the earth, that means I'm dead. And if I'm room temperature, then who's driving my truck? I really don't want my brother-in-law to have it.

Now let's just calm down a minute. There's got to be something we can do about this Oblivion thing.

And as it happens, I've got a humble idea. I think the only hope for our wayward nation—and I can't believe I'm saying this—is my mother-in-law. That's right, she's going to save us from Yankee Oblivion.

We're going to start a Southern school, and my mother-in-law will be the dean. If you've never met her, she speaks like a jar of unrefrigerated Karo syrup. She uses words like, "WUN-dah-ful," and, "simply MAH-vah-luss."

Yes, here at Southern Academic Speech School, ("S.A.S.S."), Mother Mary promises to teach authentic Southern dialect. And, kids will learn other Southern values too; how to write thank-you cards, proper koozie etiquette, and how to dump peanuts into Coca-Cola (Ko-KOLA).

For morning exercises: students recite the Lord's Prayer in five different languages. Georgian, Alabamian, Mississippian, Good Ol' Boy, and Methodist. Students also dine on Southern cuisine. For breakfast: grits (GREE-yits), biscuits (BEE-skitts), and sausage links (Conecuh). For lunch: a tomato sandwich ('mater-sammich), slathered with mayonnaise (Duke's), and a healthy beverage (Bud Lite).

At the academy, we hereby foreswear to preach old-fashioned values. We'll teach your children to appreciate trucks, Blue Tick hounds, Georgia Pacific paper products, Bear Bryant, Shug Jordan, and pound cake.

Either that, or I'm packing my bags and moving to cotton-picking Oblivion.

Because my brother-in-law is not getting my truck.

# POLITICAL

A woman attacked me in Winn Dixie. Then, without warning, she served me a glossy political brochure and hummed a few bars of "God Bless America." After a swat on my hindsection, she then pounced on the next unsuspecting idiot in the checkout line.

Well, it will come as no shock to know that I have strong political convictions. Big ones. And I'll share them with you, if I may. After all, I'm the one writing.

This year, I'm voting for overcooked collard greens, butterbeans, and creamed corn. The kind with so much butter you can develop a stroke just sniffing the skillet.

Also, tomatoes and cucumbers—which are technically bipartisan fruits. Because I love fruit. Not the kind in cans. That stuff tastes like pickled gallbladders.

I'm talking about the fruit you only get south of Macon County. Peaches tender enough to make a grown man pee himself. On a long drive, I've eaten so many gushing peaches before, I had to change my shirt twice.

Also, I'm in favor of our God-given right to deep fry. Which I freely exercise. Without it we'd be a nation on the skids. Because the only thing separating us from heathens, is our fried catfish.

Furthermore: there are no rules to frying. In fact, with the right batter, it's permissible to fry your own boot— which I've seen done once. That was one drunk groom.

I hope wheat flour makes the ballot. Modern health extremists say gluten will transform our brains into Fluffernutter. But I support bread.

I knew an old man who said once, "We were so poor, Mama only ever had one bag of flour, and a jar of hog grease. Each morning, when I prayed for Daily Bread, by God, I meant bread."

How's that for a campaign slogan?

I'd rather eat bread than talk politics. I'd rather drown my plate in giblet gravy and fall asleep on the sofa. If you think that's un-American, get in line.

I believe in sweet corn, ripe enough to eat raw. And yams, suffocated in butter. Barbecue shoulder, fat tomatoes, Andersonville peaches, and giant drumsticks.

Give us this day our Daily Biscuits, oh Lord. And, if it's not too much trouble.

Teach me to love.

# BIG OLD BOYS

I saw him a few months ago, with his son, at a barbecue joint in Middle Alabama. A place that serves spicy pulled pork sandwiches big enough to qualify as real estate.

His son had grown even taller than his daddy, which is saying something. His daddy is no shorty. When I pumped the boy's skillet-sized hand, It was hard not to feel like a river shrimp.

I remember when my wife used to babysit this freckle-face, he was no bigger than a Twinkie back then. Now, he's a six-foot-seven man. Not a freckle on him.

His daddy and I suffered through the awkward Gosh-I-Dont-Know-How-We-Lost-Touch ritual—both of us exaggerating how busy we've been. When the truth is, some folks aren't meant to be friends for more than a few summers. I asked how his wife was getting along.

He hung his head. "Well, you must've heard, Sylvia's dying."

You could've knocked me over with a stiff breeze.

Sylvia—which is not her name—is a woman in her

mid-forties with white-blonde hair and a warm helping of personality. She led the Women's Prayer Group. Because, you see, Sylvia is a Baptist more sincere than a locust-and-honey sandwich.

She's no stranger to malignant things, either. She must've prayed for a million folks in her time. Sometimes her prayers whipped cancer into remission. Other times, not.

Her own fate; one of the latter instances.

"We prayed the Lord would heal her," said her husband. "But, it's been a long fight. Well... That is... When God takes her home..."

No sooner had he said it than his son buried his own head into his jacket. I tried not to stare at the boy while he choked on his tears. Besides, the kid's a man now. It's impolite to stare at a man who's sobbing. Even though the fella is the size of a live oak tree.

After a few minutes, the boy sniffed and said, "I'm sorry I cried like that, sir."

No you're not, son.

Don't be sorry. And next time, don't stop crying until you're good and ready. She's your mama.

She deserves every ever-loving tear you've got.

# YOUR FIRST DOG

I received a question yesterday from a boy named Robert: "Dear Mister Sean, my mom told me to ask you if you think I should buy a dog. I'll be nine March."

Firstly, Robert, you have an impressively wise mother. Secondly: you've done the right thing coming to me, since I have extensive, immeasurable knowledge in this field.

See Robert, every dog-loving stiff knows pet ownership changes your life. No longer can you do the things you used to. Things like eat, sleep, think, pay taxes, or watch television.

Imagine: you settle down to watch Sesame Street. You prop your feet up, crack open a Budweiser, and let out a satisfied sigh. But as soon as you do, your dog begins to suffer serious bladder pains.

And even though Cookie Monster is in classic form today, your pet's urinary system just hit red-level. And now he's a threat to your mom's living room.

Your dog starts whining in a way that sounds like your grandmother fell in the shower.

"Hush!" you'll shout.

But finally, you'll get up and open the door. He'll run outside, lift his leg, and unleash the Mississippi.

"Good boy," you'll say. "Come, back inside, Sesame Street's on!"

But hold your horses, Robert. Why are you always in such a hurry? There's an odor in your backyard that wasn't there ten minutes ago. It's probably nothing. But your dog comes from a long line of drug-detecting animals. He needs to investigate.

You shut the door.

You sit down again. And as soon as you do; loud scratching. And if you ignore this, your dog will do the old-lady-with-a-broken-hip scream again.

Thus, you'll invite him inside, and I think you see where I'm going here. This is dog ownership, Robert. You sit down. The dog whines. You get up. Door opens. Door closes. Barking. Door opens. Closes again. Barking.

Eventually, you'll get tired of his routine and call your dog's bluff. Then, he'll wander into your kitchen and bluff his brains out all over the floor.

So, to answer your question, Robert: no, I do not think you should buy a dog.

You should buy two.

# DIXIE KIDS

If you ask a bunch of children about the current state of American politics, you're bound to have some kids begin drawing on themselves with magic markers. Likely, you'll have to repeat the question.

"I think," yelled five-year-old, Taylor. "America should have a big billboard that says: 'We Love Everybody.' Well, unless they're bad guys. Because, God told us to love other people and not hit our brother."

Taylor's little brother nodded in hearty agreement.

"Not me," said six-year-old Martin. "I think we should do waterslides, tall ones, so even all the poor little kids can slide, up and down, and they fall into the pool thingy, below. Yes. Because that's America to me."

I was glad to discover Martin shared my political-views. Sliding up and down, falling into pool thingies, these are longstanding American traditions.

"My dad says," shouted Taylor's four-year-old brother. "We're not supposed to eat our boogers, they'll make us sick!"

His sister set the record straight. "He did NOT say

that, MOM did," and then Taylor slugged her brother, violating the sixth commandment.

A little redheaded girl chimed in, "America is where land is free, and the braves are home!"

Close enough.

"My dad, loves the Atlanta Braves," said one boy.

"They're the greatest!" said another.

"Everybody calm down," I said. "Besides, everyone knows the Braves went downhill when they lost Bobby Cox."

"I think," added a mild-mannered boy missing his front teeth. "America should do the big thing, you know, like, when we did that time, and everyone danced..."

"You'll have to speak up," I said. "I didn't quite catch that."

So he used broad hand gestures. "Sometimes when I try to swing my arms..."

"Okay."

"...And then I'm like this."

"Right."

The tallest girl in the bunch said, "My daddy's coming home in two weeks after being overseas a long time. We're waiting to celebrate my birthday until he's back."

"How long's he been gone?"

"Almost a year, he's in the Air Force, does that count? I mean, is that American stuff?"

Yes, honey.

It's the most American stuff there is.

# MARITAL BLISS

I don't mean to criticize, but the marriage books you're supposed to read before you waltz down the aisle are a waste of seventy-two dollars. Take me, for instance. Every time I've used Dr. Noah Fence's recommended New York Times Bestselling catchphrase —"How's your love-tank, sweetie?"—I get a bloody lip and end up sleeping in my truck.

And then one day, while resting my head against the steering wheel, I came up with the secret to marital bliss. Which I've cleverly entitled: The Secret to Marital Bliss.

Fatty food.

Exhibit A: Lucky for me, our first apartment sat two hundred feet from a pizza joint. The kind of place operated by hormonal teenagers who sneak off to taste each other's braces in the walk-in cooler.

Whenever Jamie and I started fussing, I'd bolt. I'd trot straight to the pizza joint and shout, "Get out of the freezer! You have a customer!" Thus, some kid with a hickie would make me a large pie, I'd be back home in six minutes.

Jamie would see the box, smile and say, "What took you so long, jackass?" And somehow, I'd know we were going to be okay.

After one slice, she'd lose her black pointy hat and stop referring to our dogs as "my pretties." And then she'd say, "You should watch baseball tonight, love bug."

To which I'd answer, "No, let's watch Lifetime again, cheek-whistle."

"No, baseball."

"Lifetime."

"Baseball."

Then we'd passionately kiss like teenagers in a walk-in cooler, until God sent his angels to break up the party —because this is a family story.

So, once you harness the marital power of artery-clogging food, marriage will be a picnic. In fact, I've based every home purchase around corresponding restaurants. You think I'm joking? I never joke.

America is full of starving couples who spend too much time arguing because of low blood sugar. They wander the streets with sour looks on their faces, headed for the Big D—and I don't mean Decatur. This is because they haven't tasted sausage in a decade.

Look, I'm all in favor of eating ultra-healthy things, believe me. And by all means, eat your broccoli.

But you'd better get used to sleeping in your truck, big boy.

# BETTER

Not that you would care, but I thought he was a genius. I'll call him Zeek. And the things Zeek could do with pork shoulders made even devout Baptists use exclamatory cuss words.

"Damn, Zeek, that's good," someone might say. And I've cleaned up the language considerably. My mother reads these things.

Old Zeek was as smokey as the grill he worked behind; two fifty-gallon drums welded together, on wheels. The thing sat in a parking lot behind the supermarket. And every Saturday, he muddied up ten miles of air with hickory smoke. Barbecue aficionados like me could get as much hog as we could stand.

Or, you were welcome to sit beneath the shade with him, listening to him talk. Which he was glad to do.

"You should'a been alive fifty years ago," he said once. "White folk never gave us the time of day, if'n you was a ni—" He stopped himself, but I knew what word came next.

"Matter of fact," said Zeek. "In my daddy's day, black

111

folk was nothing. Juss nothing."

"What do you mean?"

"Means my daddy knowed what it was like to get whooped on."

"For real?"

"Yes, for real," he said. "At one time, it was no crime to strike a black man. 'Course, you's too young to even know what I'm talking about."

Thank God for that.

"Things got worse, too," Zeek went on. "When I got older, the world changed." He made his eyes big. "Riots everywhere. 'Lotta hate during that time. Lucky you's born after all that."

Lucky me.

"But," he said, "It ain't like that no more. Everything's getting better."

"Better, really?"

"Yessir. Did you know my daughter is a nurse? Long ago, that would'a never happened."

"Yeah, but things aren't really better."

"Yes, they are. This world's gettin' more loving. No matter what you hear on TV, there's 'lotta strong folks been fightin' for love since before we got here." He winked. "We believe in love, that it has power to change the world."

Well, I understand Zeek passed a few years ago. But there's something I want to say, if he's listening out there:

I hope you're right, sir.

# MY FINAL BOW

I don't know if you've ever seen someone shoved into a bodybag, but I have. Once. It shook me.

It was at the Alabama-Georgia state line, off Interstate 85. That night, I happened upon two cars parked around a clump of smoldering steel. The driver was already dead. When the paramedics came, they removed him from the scene—in a bodybag.

The whole ordeal turned my stomach sour. I had to pull over at a gas station just to calm down. I ate four honey buns, I remember that.

Look, I'm not afraid of taking my final bow, I swear it. But what about my family? I don't want to miss out on what happens while I'm away.

And what about my hateful fifth-grade teacher? The miserable soul who flunked me. Yes, that's right, I failed the fifth cotton-picking grade. I can't die. Not yet. Because I have unfinished business with that mean little thing. I never got a chance to show her I'm not as stupid as she told me.

Or to tell her I forgive her.

Also, I can't leave my friends, the lovable fellas in my line of work; who are every bit as off-kilter as I am. Well, except Chuck. He's got us all licked.

And I'd miss my relatives, both good and bad, who've taught me things about myself—both good and bad. The fact is, I'm still learning how to be myself. I haven't mastered it yet.

I'd still like to see a few more babies, eat more ice cream cones. Or listen to more Willie Nelson songs, or get kisses on the lips by a woman who nicknamed me Fool-Ass.

If I die, that means I have to say goodbye to her. My best friend who sleeps beside me. Who's busy vacuuming the house right now. Who makes biscuits every weekend, who has perfected chicken and dumplings. Who clips the hair poking out of my ears. Whose head fits perfectly in the notch beneath my arm. I'm not afraid of bodybags. But I don't want to leave.

And I'll be frank;

I can't believe I just told you about the fifth grade.

# TOO MANY SNAKES

I just saw a snake underneath my sofa and almost made a little mess in my britches. The thing zigged and zagged like Lucifer himself. Luckily, however, I know exactly what to do in these dire situations.

1: Remain calm.

2: Lock yourself in the pantry and set your couch on fire.

"What are we going to do?" my wife asked.

"We?" I said. " You're on your own. I'm moving to Canada."

"Sweetie, come down from the refrigerator and get the garden hoe like a real, strapping man."

Listen here, I'm a strapping man. As a matter of fact, I go strapping all the time. Sometimes, twice a day. But no amount of strapping can make me like snakes. I hate them so much I can't even finish reading this. I'm sorry, you'll just have to keep going without me.

The Associated Press reported that snakes are "taking over" the South. Those are the exact words from the article: "taking over." As opposed to, say, "migrating

South," or, "building summer cottages in Orange Beach."

Last year, local governments deputized six hundred snake-hunters to handle the crisis. But don't get your hopes up. After a year of snake killing in Alabama, Georgia, and Florida, hunters only managed to kill a mere sixty-one.

Well shrimp my grits.

I don't mean to complain, but I can kill at least seventy cottonmouths just backing out of my driveway. What's going on here? I'm no statistician, but can't six hundred men with shotguns kill at least enough snakes to fill a shoebox? I don't want to blow this out of proportion, but this is the most serious crisis facing North America.

I wish I were kidding, but I'm as serious as a milkshake. Pardon my math, but Ophiologists predict migrating snakes will blanket twenty-four thirds of Alabama and Florida within the next ten minutes. We're talking thirty-three-foot pythons that strangle Teddy bears just for kicks. Some of these things tip the scales at two hundred pounds and have names like, Albert, or Justin.

As it turns out, Albert is a lot faster than your wife is with her garden hoe.

Or your mother-in-law.

Or your aunt, Flossie.

# WALTON COUNTY BOYS

Our Paxton boys played ball. In fact, it was the best basketball the little city has seen since the mid-seventies. That is, if you can call Paxton a city.

Most folks have never visited a place as small as Paxton, Florida. A town within spitting distance of Alabama. At the moment, there are 706 residents here—unless, God forbid, someone's granny dies. And this year's senior class isn't big enough to fill up a few church vans.

Paxton is four miles wide, with a town-hall about the size of a Tom Thumb. Most of the people living here skate along the poverty threshold. And most of these hardworking folks don't even know what that is exactly. Or care. At least not this week.

Because this week, their boys played white-hot basketball.

The Paxton Bobcats took the court in Lakeland, Florida, while half the town sat in the bleachers with hand-painted signs.

These are the state championships. The singular

biggest event some of these country kids will ever see—besides their own weddings. The boys were full of syrup-thick adrenaline. Each of them smiled big enough to see their teeth from the nosebleed section. They might as well have been in the NBA finals.

The first half: wiry Zach Varnum guided the Bobcats to a joyous lead. He's liquid dynamite. There's no doubt about it, this kid's going places. Each time one of these athletes made a play, I understand the auditorium of mamas almost ripped the room apart—which is what mamas do.

But after halftime, the winds changed and everything went south. The Paxton boys clawed with everything they had. The other team clawed harder.

When the game was over, the boys sat disappointed, slumping their shoulders. But their mamas weren't about to let them get away with such behavior. Because heroes don't sulk. Besides, these champions have already made an entire city—no the entire county —proud.

The fact is, this is the 1A State Championship, and our rural Walton County boys were there, by God. They played their cotton-picking hearts out. And they'll remember this blessed day forever. Nobody's mama gives a cuss about the final score.

And neither do we.

# WE ARE GOING TO DIE

If you're reading this, I'm dead. Or: trapped beneath a pile of softball-sized hail, wearing a bike helmet. My wife saw on television that bike helmets protect against tornadoes and various airborne sixteen-wheelers. I guess she was wrong. Since I'm dead.

Anyway, I'm not going to mince words, the weather is ugly right now, folks.

While I write this, it sounds like the outside world is about to explode. My mother-in-law is looking out the window in horror—she's wearing my old catcher's mask and chest protector. And I can't help but wonder if she'd be able to handle my four-seam fastball with that new hip of hers.

Earlier today, emergency officials recommended stockpiling a disaster survival kit, which I've already done. Flashlight, candles, lighter, radio, coffee, Southern Living cookbooks, and a sterilized five-gallon bucket with a toilet seat.

Also: toilet paper. Even in dire situations, we only buy quilted Tempurpedic tissue. The last time I bought the cheap stuff, Jamie used it for sanding oil stains on the driveway.

So, make no mistake about it, we're all going die. Helmets and all. If you don't believe me, just watch the news coverage. They'll convince you in only three seconds.

The multicolored weather maps are downright apocalyptic. The green-colored areas, (marginal risk zones) are where it's raining twenty inches. The orange areas (enhanced risk zones), twenty-five inches. The red areas (write-your-will-on-a-paper-towel-zones), are where chunks of Alabama and Florida get sucked into outer space.

And, just in case viewers' underpants are still clean, the weatherman plays footage of Hurricane Andrew, Hugo, Katrina, and Iwo Jima to remind us of what we're dealing with.

Disaster authorities advise taking shelter in a concrete place, like the garage. Which is what we're doing right now.

The three of us have made camp next to my beer fridge. My wife and mother-in-law each get their own cot and sleeping bag; I'm huddled next to the lawnmower for warmth. But the truth is, it doesn't matter. According to the weatherman, we'll all be dead in a few hours anyway.

When you find my body, if you'd be kind enough to promise me something:

Don't tell anyone about this stupid helmet.

# UGLY AS SIN

You're not ugly. I don't know who you are, but you need to hear that. Because the world is telling you otherwise. I know this because the world's telling me the same thing.

It's in every television commercial, Victoria's Secret ad, music video, and magazine. For Christ's sake, look at our movie stars, they're plastic.

Oscars week is here, and if you want to see what's wrong with society, watch celebrities walk the red carpet. Reporters will nitpick four-thousand-dollar outfits. Entire conversations will circulate around a dress that has its own Facebook page. Meanwhile: somewhere in Africa, a toddler sleeps in a cardboard box, drinking his own toilet water.

Well, I don't give a Funyun what celebrities wear to their bar mitzvahs. I care even less who has the nicest-looking pair of hindcheeks. The truth is, Hollywood cares more about us than we do about them.

Don't believe me? You should. Celebrities spend millions advertising themselves. They want you—need you—to love them. If you don't, they're unemployed. So, they'll wear whatever they need to get your attention, or by God, they'll go buck naked.

In the end, it's children who suffer. Because girls aren't supposed to have the cartoonish figure of Kim Kardashian.

A 2015 study discovered that girls below age fourteen are ten times more likely to develop eating disorders than two decades ago. And it's not just girls. The same study shows a staggering percentage of boys have anorexia and bulimia, too.

What is happening to us?

I remember when we boys would eat ourselves until we passed out behind the shed. When all red-blooded teenagers practically sold themselves into slavery for ice cream.

So, I'll say it again, in case you didn't understand me. You're not fat. You're not average. You're not stupid, muffin-topped, dog-faced, pale, boring, nerdy, or anything else.

You're a magnolia, made to be exactly the way you are. It doesn't get any more authentic than you. You're the real thing. Those celebrities you're watching, with caked on makeup, who've insured their hindparts for more than my house is worth; they're the fakes. I don't care what anyone tells you.

You are not ugly.

And that means you.

# CHIPLEY FLORIDA TRAINS

The train whistle screamed so loud I had to plug my ears. It was the kind of sound that made every face in Chipley, Florida light up like Christmas trees.

The man next to me shouted, "Lordy mercy!"

If you've never been to Chipley, you don't know what you're missing. And if you're just riding through town, it lasts about as long as a George Jones song. On a good day, you can stand on one side of Chipley, let out holler, and they'll hear you on the other side.

Chipley is the county seat for Washington, County. A tiny county with not enough residents to fill up one fifth of an SEC football stadium. It's a dry county. And if you don't know what that is, watch an episode of the Andy Griffith show. Mayberry was a dry town.

Chipley had a courthouse that screamed 1930—a block building with tall columns. There's a downtown, one you could roll a bowling ball through without any effort. The biggest buildings here are churches—which remind me of potlucks and revival meetings.

The most important event on the calendar, besides

Easter Sunday, is the Watermelon Festival. A summer shindig that attracts professional people-watchers from all over the tri-county region. Take me, for instance, I am a professional people-watcher.

Last year at the festival, I saw a man with a skunk perched on his shoulder. Beside him, his wife and two kids, each with stink badgers of their own. "They make great pets." he said. "Better than expensive purebreds." His wife agreed. His boys were too busy working on funnel cakes to comment.

So you can imagine how stunning it was to see Chipley's train station fire up again for the first time in years. No, it was more than stunning, it was Mayberry. The crowd gathered to watch the metal machine roll in. Chipley folks grinned at the train, hoping Amtrak chooses to reinstate an old route.

"Lordy Mercy!" the man said, elbowing me. "Looky!"

The old depot, which stood for 134 years in the same blessed spot before being torn down, would've remained unimpressed by the modern train. The ghost-station had seen enough locomotives and wartime departures to get worked up anymore.

But we the people came unglued.

"I seen them working on them tracks," said the excited Chipley man beside me. "Lordy mercy, I hope it means they're fixin' to get this train up and rolling again. That would mean everything to our little community. We need all the help we can get."

He's absolutely right, of course. Small towns are disappearing at alarming rates, changing into something else. It's a nationwide issue. The town I grew up in erected a Red Lobster over my second base. I spent half my childhood punching my glove in the same spot the dumpster now sits. There's a Best Buy over my spaceship fort. A Dick's Sporting Goods over the place where I had my first kiss.

There's something about a train station that flies in the face of Red Lobsters and Best Buys. I don't know why the sound of a whistle makes me proud of things like high school football games, or Sadie Hawkins dances. Or dry counties.

But Lordy mercy.

I hope they get that train up and rolling again.

# SOUTHERN BELLES

If you're a boy, and you're thinking of marrying a Southern woman like I did, you'd do well to understand how she thinks first.

Take, for instance, my wife, Jamie. I've spent years in training beneath her tutelage. I've learned a few things. Not a lot, but a little.

And I'd like to share some tips to help you on your journey, my friend.

1: Even though your Southern wife appreciates you trying, you are much too simpleminded to wash dishes. In fact, you couldn't even make ice without a recipe. Loading residential dishwashers is only to be done by card-carrying members of the Junior League—or their mothers.

2: Do your wife a favor and familiarize yourself with the federal laws of Southern female fashion. They aren't difficult to remember. Here's one: females shall not wear white between Labor Day and the SEC Championship. Unless it's a leap year. In which case, women are not allowed to wear chevron-print, flip flops, corduroy, or expose tattoos to members of the Rotary Club on Tuesdays.

3: Grocery lists can be fun. Lists written by your Southern wife will contain cryptic shorthand only intelligible to certain members of Navajo tribes. Furthermore, you're a terrible supermarket shopper. All that cheap toilet paper you bought? Your wife could sand a boat with that stuff.

4: At night, it is permitted for a Southern woman's bedside lamp to remain on while she catches up on Russian Literature. Yes, it might seem as though you're falling asleep with aircraft lights aimed at your wispy thin eyelids. You can always try cussing.

5: Remember the good old days? When you used to tell stories to buddies, and they'd die with laughter? That's over now. A Southern debutante like your wife has legal authority to question your bull-hockey in public. Once she shuts you down, she will then prove that you don't even know how to spell debutante.

6: You used to pick out your own clothes. Nowadays, you couldn't dress a scarecrow worth a cuss.

7: Always remember that your honey-do list will be written on your tombstone and in your obituary. Your mother-in-law already knows this list backward and forward. So do members of your local Junior League chapter.

8: When out for dinner, it is grounds for divorce to order a salad if your Dixie Belle orders steak, pork, or chitlins. She will think you are making a passive aggressive statement and confront you with, "Salad? Are you trying to say I'm a fat-ass?" Similarly, never, under any circumstances, go to the gym together.

9: If you should ever eat peanut butter with a spoon, please see *rule number 1.*

10: When your Southern wife asks, "Do I look fat?" any response (including involuntary twitches of your trick eyelid) will be your last. Try this: tuck a five-dollar bill into her waistband, then tell her to walk slowly around the room while you holler and whistle like a fool.

However, if your wife is like mine, she won't even bat an eyelash for anything less than a fifty.

# YOUR GUIDE TO SOUTHERN TRAVEL

If you're taking a vacation to the Deep South, and you're not from our neck of the woods—meaning you say things like, "you guys," or, "soda pop," or, "so is your old man,"—you might need a translator.

Thus, I'd like to offer you my mother-in-law. Because you won't find anyone more Southern than her. Besides, I need something to write about. These things don't just write themselves, you know.

Anyway, Mary has reasonable rates. And if you pack a cooler with a few cucumber sandwiches, she'll ride with you all the way to the Czech Republic if need be. She'll even help drive. But not at night—cataracts.

A few things before we get started: you'll need to give Mary her B-12 injections. Also, make sure she takes her meds with each meal. But don't worry, I'll send handwritten instructions along with her oxygen tanks and walker.

And away you go.

Let's assume you start your trip in a Godless Northern city like, oh I don't know, Cincinnati. This is a good place to start. Because from here, it'll only take a few minutes to cross the Mason Dixon Line into Kentucky.

Ready, set, go.

After a long time in your minivan, rolling past various Kentucky things, like mountains, you'll hit Bowling Green. Here, you can wake Mary up from her nap. You're going to need her from here on out. Because even though you aren't really that far from your gray, dismal home, you're lightyears away from your Yankee comfort zone.

For example: when you ask directions at the dilapidated service station, from a fella named Jay Jay.

Jay Jay says, "Turn lef' rye' chair, at duh rett latt."

It's a good thing you have Mary. She speaks fluent Kentuckian.

"D'rectly 'head?" she restates. "The rett latt, up yondah?" She says it like she was born in the hills of the Bluegrass State, with a silver banjo in her mouth.

"Yessum. Rye 'chonder. This road's fixin' to lead y'all to Inna-State Sitty-Fav."

"Oh, wunduhfull," says Mary. "We 'preciate it."

Jay Jay tips his ball cap and gives the universal Southern farewell blessing, "Y'all be safe."

Your ears are worn out, and you're still trying to figure out what "Yessum," means.

Aren't you glad you hired Mary?

Once you cross the Kentucky-Tennessee border, you'll zip past Portland, White House, and Millersville. And when you're well into Tennessee, reach behind your seat and get Mary a cucumber sandwich. She's got the shakes.

After more hours of driving, you'll hit Nashville.

Home of aerosol hairspray and very optimistic poor people.

Nashville is a unique city indeed. To put it in terms Cincinnattians understand: pretend Las Vegas and Disney World had a baby that came out shaped like a neon guitar with big hair. And this little neon thing is trying like hell to win American Idol. That's Nashville.

Keep driving.

When you hit Franklin, Mary's hungry again. That cucumber sandwich wasn't enough to say grace over. Off the beaten path, is Puckett's Grocery Store. Stop there. It's a tin shed that serves things like cherry smoked ribs, fried dill pickles, and whole catfish. You'll thank Mary for suggesting such a place. Your cardiologist will cuss you. But this this the South. We all cuss a little bit.

When you sit at your table, your server's accent will be thick as clay. Just let Mary do all the talking.

The waitress asks in Tennessean—making each word she says last roughly two seconds, "Hi y'all doin' t'day?"

"Fann," Mary says, browsing the menu, drawing *her* word out for a whole five seconds. "Mighty fann, fann. We juss' fann. How 'bout you?"

"Oh, fann, fann, I'm fann, thanks."

"Oh, that's fann," says Mary.

Once Mary has determined that everyone in the direct circumference is, in fact, fine; and that no stories about the time she went to Huntingdon College and met a tennis player who looked an awful lot like Rock Hudson need to be told for social levity, we can get on with ordering.

The waitress says, "Y'all won't tea?"

"Ma'am?" Mary asks, cupping her ear. She forgot her hearing aids in the minivan.

"Tea," the girl repeats. "Y'all won't ass tea?"

Of course Mary wants tea—with extra ass, please. And you want some, too. However, this is Tennessee, not Ohio. Tea is different here. Mary advises *you* skip the tea because you're not ready for it yet. It takes years to build up a tolerance for this much sugar. Your teeth are liable to rot out and fall into your basket of fried chicken gizzards.

Order an "ass water" instead.

After a greasy lunch, it's back to the interstate. Mary would like to listen to some Hank Williams music. If you don't know who that is, don't worry. She brought CDs in her handbag. Make sure she has her hearing aids in, or she'll blow your stereo speakers.

The Tennessee highway will lull you through a rolling landscape. When you hit Columbia, Mary directs you to Highway 31, which winds through microscopic towns not big enough to have mailboxes. This is God's country. Where freezers sit on front porches; where hamburger come made of deer meat—and so do family memories. Learn to appreciate it instead of criticizing it. These are good people.

The exact moment you cross the Tennessee-Alabama line, Mary will instruct you to lift your feet.

"Yay," she hollers.

Isn't she fun?

"Yay," you say in a monotone voice. "Why are we lifting our feet?"

Because, Mister Cincinnati, you've just entered Alabama the Beautiful, Mary's home state. Now pull over. She's ten minutes past due for a B-12 injection. Give it to her in the shoulder. And make sure she closes her eyes, or she'll see you coming with the syringe and tense up so hard she'll bend the needle.

Once in the Yellowhammer State, you'll drive past Athens and Tanner, enjoying the absence of skyscrapers, and other various god-awful ugly things common to Cincinnati. Mary suggests you spend the night in Decatur—a town on the majestic Tennessee River.

When you check in to the roadside motel, you know the drill. Let Mary handle conversation with the natives.

"Haddy dew?" says the night clerk. "Way y'all frum?"

"Rye' cheer," Mary says, in Alabamian.

He looks once at Mary. Then, at your auspicious L.L. Bean jacket and ironed blue jeans. "Hmmmm. What 'bout him? He don't look like he's frum 'round these parts."

"Him?" Mary smiles. Drawing on her training as a substitute teacher, she knows an Alabamian phrase which covers a multitude of Yankee sins. "That's because he's from Huntsville."

The night clerk grins. "Oh, Huntsville? N'that case, I reckon y'all can have the in-state discount."

And just like that, Mary saved you two hundred dollars. Now go help her set up her oxygen machine. Make sure to wear the back-brace I packed for you. That thing weighs as much as a bird bath.

After a good night's sleep, you wake bright and early. And, like any self-reliant Cincinnatian, it only takes you a few minutes to pack your car, iron your underpants, and eat whatever it is Yankees eat for breakfast. But slow down, Mister Big City. Mary hasn't finished her fourteen-plate breakfast yet. This is the South, the most important meal of the day is right now. Pass the syrup, please. And the jam. And the honey.

This coffee needs sugar.

Are you going to finish your pancakes?

Back on the road.

Mary instructs you to keep on the interstate. Pass Falkville, Cullman, Smoke Rise, and Kimberly. This is a gorgeous drive, where the grassy pastures look so green, they're almost Navy blue. And if you can't find pleasure in this, drive slower.

Outside Birmingham, take Highway 20. Ride past Fairfield, Midfield, and lots of other big fields. Once you reach the nothing-of-a-town called Cottondale, it won't be long before you see the welcome-sign for Tuscaloosa.

Welcome to town.

Now you're screwed.

This is stand-still traffic. Mary forgot to tell you, tonight is the University of Alabama's big football game. They're playing Georgia tonight. Which means heaven and earth pause momentarily while God inhabits the body of a man named Nick Saban.

There are so many cars on the highway, you can't see a stitch of asphalt. You're going to be stuck for a while. You might as well get yourself a cucumber sandwich and a cold beer.

To help pass the time, Mary tells you a story about how her grandaddy once bought a mule, and how he taught it to walk it in a straight-line, as opposed to circles, and how her mother, blah blah blah. You don't care.

Still, even though her story seems like a boring one, Mary knows how to make the tale—provided there are no interruptions—last until the end of time.

Smile and pretend to listen, look out your window and take in the magnificent college town. It's is a marvelous place, made up almost entirely of the color testosterone. Count yourself lucky to see this place on game day, in all its glory. There's enough electricity in the air to power a streetcar.

You'll note, on this historically crucial game night —all game nights are historically crucial game nights— folks in town think only about two things: (a) winning, (b) not losing.

One is more important than the other.

Quick! Look out your windshield. See up there? That college kid is mooning you from a fourth-story balcony. His hindcheeks are painted with two big red A's. That boy is a state-sanctioned ambassador of our great Alabama territory. He's not even drunk yet.

Mary sees him.

"Oh, how *mahvelous*," she says. "One of our ambassadors."

She might be in her seventies, but she likes a good pair of ambassadors as much as the next gal.

Once you get out of the congested town, Highway 20 takes you across Alabama, into Mississippi. Here, you'll notice the air grows increasingly humid. By the time you get to Hattiesburg, Mary's mule story ought to be reaching intermission.

Hop out and stretch your legs. Take the opportunity to stay at Sunny Grove Bed and Breakfast—

an old house that looks like it it's survived eight Civil Wars. Bed and breakfasts are one of the South's trademarks.

Take extra care when you set up Mary's oxygen machine tonight. Last night, you connected a hose wrong, and she almost choked to death. Don't forget your back brace.

Next morning: more driving.

As soon as your tires touch the highway, Mary resumes her mule story. By now, you've learned how to induce yourself into a zombie-like trance by humming just quiet enough not to be heard by fine-tuned hearing aids. And, you've already spiked your coffee with Irish whiskey. Congratulations, you're getting more Southern by the minute, big boy.

And then you hit New Orleans.

No sooner do you cross the city boundary than someone hands you a plastic pitcher of beer and a handful of beads.

The air here is salty enough to taste. The streets, so diverse and bright, they make Paris look like a joke. And with Mary translating, you explore the French Quarter like a seasoned professional.

You see cobblestoned streets, gas lanterns, and flamboyant locals—easily spotted by the handguns tucked in their waistbands. The atmosphere of this odd place, awakens something inside you that feels an awful lot like you have to pee. That beer you just guzzled has to go somewhere.

So.

You do what all New Orleans locals do, you find an empty alley to take care of business. While you're concentrating, a fella wearing only one shoe removes your wallet, helps himself to your cash, then makes a snide remark about your driver's license photo.

Then, you wander onto Magazine Street, someone throws a beer bottle at you, and miraculously, it doesn't break. Which makes you want another beer. On Bourbon Street, the world is already spinning like a merry-go-round. There, a man walking on stilts calls you a name rhyming with "sugar wussy," and then hands you a flier with a naked woman on it. All you do is laugh and say, "Do you know where versutable selndor were sonder wanna go?"

Time for another beer.

Anyway, I think it's best if we end our trip here. Besides, you're too drunk to go any further. And this was supposed to be a family story. You've turned it into something not fit for network television.

Thus, when your vacation is over, make certain you pay my mother-in-law generously for her services. She's worked hard giving you your money's worth. Besides, it's no cakewalk keeping someone who irons their blue jeans entertained for several hours in a minivan. And even though you might not know it, you got a real discount.

She must like you.

Her mule stories usually costs extra.

# ME IN MY OWN WORDS

As a child, I liked to write. I filled up notebooks with tales of the high-seas, shameless vixens, and steamy scenarios combining both of the aforementioned. My fifth grade teacher found one of my notebooks and scanned through it. She told me I wrote with too many commas, and encouraged me to pursue a career in construction work.

That, old, woman, never, liked, me.

Years later, I learned my teacher had left the school. She took a job at the Piggly Wiggly as a cashier. I went to visit the old girl, to show her the man I'd grown into.

She seemed genuinely glad to see me. And I was just as glad to find her wearing that red apron for a living. After visiting for a few minutes, I realized something I'd never noticed before. Beneath her hardshell exterior was a regular lady, working from nine to five for pennies. She was doing the best she could with her life. Just like me.

Before I left, she asked me what kind of work I did.

At the time, I worked in construction.

## SEAN DIETRICH

*Sean Dietrich is a writer, humorist, and novelist, known for his commentary on life in the American South. His humor and short fiction appear in various publications throughout the Southeast, including* South Magazine, *the* Tallahassee Democrat, Wired Magazine, Food Network Blog, Outdoors Magazine, *and he is a member of the NWU. His first short story was published during childhood, in a hometown journal newspaper. Since then, he's pursued his literary interests authoring four novels, writing humor, and short stories.*

*An avid sailor and fisherman, when he's not writing, he spends much of his time aboard his sailboat* (The S.S. Squirrel)*, riding the Gulf of Mexico, along with his coonhound, Ellie Mae.*

FOR MORE STORIES, OR TO CONTACT SEAN, VISIT:
**WWW.SEANOFTHESOUTH.COM**

Made in United States
Orlando, FL
12 December 2023

40719502R00088